CREATIVE CONTAINER GARDENING

150 Recipes for Baskets, Tubs and Window Boxes

GARDENING

150 Recipes for Baskets, Tubs and Window Boxes

*Kathleen Brown and
Effie Romain*

MICHAEL JOSEPH
LONDON

MICHAEL JOSEPH LTD

Published by the Penguin Group
27 Wrights Lane, London W8 5TZ, England
Viking Penguin Inc., 40 West 23rd Street, New York, New York 10010, USA
Penguin Books Australia Ltd, Ringwood, Victoria, Australia
Penguin Books Canada Ltd, 2801 John Street, Markham, Ontario, Canada L3R 1B4

Penguin Books (NZ) Ltd, 182-190 Wairau Road, Auckland 10, New Zealand

Penguin Books Ltd, Registered Offices: Harmondsworth, Middlesex, England

First published in Great Britain in April 1987
Second impression November 1987
First published in Mermaid Books in March 1988
Second impression November 1988

© Text 1987 by Kathleen Brown and Effie Romain
© Photographs 1987 by Tim Woodcock
© Line Illustrations 1987 by Yvonne Skargon

British Library Cataloguing in Publication Data

Brown, Kathleen
Creative container gardening: 150 recipes for baskets, tubs
and window boxes.
1. Container gardening
I. Title   II. Romain, Effie
635'.048   SB418

ISBN 0-7181-2732-3 (hardback)
ISBN 0-7181-3034-0 (paperback)

Typeset in England by The Burlington Press (Cambridge) Ltd
Printed in Spain by Artes Gráficas Toledo, S.A.
D.L.TO:2158-1988

CONTENTS

ACKNOWLEDGEMENTS

We wish to acknowledge the practical help and assistance of Hazel Key and her daughters Angela and Ursula of Fibrex Nurseries Ltd; Adam Caplin and Richard Jackson of The Garden Centre at Alexandra Palace; Howard and Kooiji's Nurseries, Wortham, Diss, Norfolk; Paul Rochford of Joseph Rochford Gardens, Letty Green, Herts; Ernest Russell of E.D. Russell Ltd, Edmonton and special thanks to John Taylor of O. A. Taylor and Sons Bulbs Ltd, Holbeach, Lincs.

We are very grateful to Peter Barnes, botanist at the Royal Horticultural Society, who read the text with reference to the botanical names.

We would also like to thank The Olive Trading Company Ltd, Twickenham Trading Estate, Rugby Road, Twickenham, Middlesex TW1 1DG who have lent us several of the terracotta containers and the oak trough used in this book.

Many thanks as well to the following people who have lent, housed and cared for these boxes, pots and baskets while the recipes were maturing! They include Rosamond Brown, Maureen Burrell, Jane Cooke, Gillian Dow, Pippa Cracknell, Jill Curley, Alison Dart, Basia Davey, Jane Davies, Margaret Eades, Sue Gay, Pamela Leaper, Rosalind Lewis-Williams, Barbara Manning, Jennifer McIntyre, Patricia Michelson, Joan Powell, Susan Scales, Ann Sharp, Hazel Houghton, Evelyn Wain and Pamela Walker. In addition, our thanks to Caroline Appelbe, Stephanie Darnill, Penny Hamilton and Claire Walmsley for the loan of their lawns, window ledges, and patios for photographic purposes.

But the biggest thanks go to our husbands, Simon and Michael, for all their encouragement and practical help.

LIST OF RECIPES

PERENNIAL RECIPES

AUTUMN, WINTER AND SPRING RECIPES

INTRODUCTION

Our aim in this book is to demonstrate simply, using photographs for each example, the various ways plants may be combined and successfully grown together in containers to arrive at a kind of 'live' flower arrangement. The book is designed with both the flat-dweller and the house-owner in mind, since all gardens are enhanced by the colourful focal points which containers provide.

We begin with combinations of perennials and shrubs. Once planted, some of the perennial recipes can be left undisturbed for several years: the evergreens provide year round interest; the deciduous shrubs mark out the seasons and the hardy perennials are a joy to watch as the first few shoots emerge in cold, wintery weather.

Next we move on to seasonal plantings. We start with ideas for Autumn, Winter and Spring, using a wide selection of dwarf bulbs. This is a time of year often neglected by container gardeners, which is a great pity because there is certainly no lack of choice. Then we come to the Summer with even more colourful examples. Many people will have tried their hand with this type of planting, but whether you have or not, there are ideas for everyone here.

We refer to our plant combinations as 'recipes'. Each one is a mixture of plant ingredients, brought together in a certain pattern and left to develop and mature. In all our recipes we give the dimensions of the container, the position most suitable for it, the time of planting, a full list of ingredients and instructions on how to plant. We then give advice on how to care for these arrangements.

You may be surprised how many bulbs and plants we use in a single display – we have found that more generous plantings give better results. We feel that each container is a feature in its own right and as such is worthy of a full planting. As long as it is well watered and fed appropriately the extra investment will have its reward.

You should be able to find most of the plants we have used at a good garden centre. If not, you can order the plants from one of the specialists listed at the back of the book. Your greengrocer is another good source. The plants he is most likely to stock include primroses, cyclamens and solanums, and perhaps some of the summer ingredients too.

PLANT NAMES
Plant names can often be a source of great confusion. Plants may be known by several different names not only in different countries but in different parts of the same country. We therefore always try to give the standard Latin name (written in italics). This is the name by which plants will be referred to in most horticultural reference books and on nurserymen's lists. We do refer to the common name where it is generally known and widely accepted, but to minimize mistakes when you come to making purchases, it is always safer to know the full Latin names.

CONTAINERS
We have used a limited selection of containers, taking the view that they are of secondary importance to the planting scheme itself. On the whole our choice has been restricted to those in common use, such as window boxes, hanging baskets, tubs, urns and chimney pots. Almost any container is suitable as long as it has drainage holes in the bottom. In some cases you will see the same container with the same evergreen framework photographed in Summer and Winter. This is intended to show you the

continuity of our recipes. Make sure that your container is clean and empty before you begin any recipe.

SOIL

Soil is most important. Unless you are familiar with making your own loam-based composts, never use ordinary garden soil. Compost, which is the name given to planting media made up to a formula, needs to have the right composition, the right amount of nutrients and to be weed-free. We generally recommend John Innes No 2 or No 3. John Innes is simply a compost formula which is sold under various different trademarks. Unfortunately the quality can vary enormously. This is sometimes due to the fact that it comes from different parts of the country but it can also be because too much clayey subsoil has been included in the mix. An alternative is to use a peat-based compost. These are much lighter and therefore suitable for hanging baskets and roof terrace work. They are also much easier to work with.

SOIL CALCULATIONS

We attempt to say how much soil will be needed in particular recipes. This is only a rough guide as there are many variables to be taken into account – we cannot know how much soil will come with each plant, for example.

As we buy our soil in litres we have used metric measurements throughout, followed by the imperial equivalent in brackets. This is a better measure for buying soil than weight because weight can be affected by moisture content.

If you are adapting our recipes to a box or trough, measure the length, width and depth in centimetres and multiply these figures to arrive at the required amount of soil.

For example:
Large Window Box
90cm (35″) long, 20cm (8″) deep, 12cm (5″) wide
Then 90 × 20 × 12 = 21600 = 21.6 litres

If you have a tub, measure the radius (ie half the diameter) and the depth. The formula is 3.14 × radius squared × depth.

For example:
Large Wooden Half Barrel
60cm (24″) in diameter, 38cm (15″) deep
The radius = ½ × 60cm = 30cm
Then
3.14 × 30 × 30 × 38 = 107388 = 107 litres

These calculations just form the basis of your estimation and will be affected by various factors. Remember to take account of the space taken by drainage material and the space left at the top of the container (a container is *never* filled with soil to the very top). Sometimes, the internal measurements of a container will differ greatly from the external ones, which again will affect the amount of soil required. And of course, soil will also come with the plants themselves – in the case of a conifer, for example, this could be quite a substantial amount.

DRAINAGE

Drainage is another essential element in container gardening. Make sure there are enough holes in the container and that they are large enough to drain properly. If you are unlucky enough to have a clayey John Innes you may find that the small holes get blocked. To avoid this use broken crocks (if you have them), gravel or horticultural grit. We have found small pieces of polystyrene invaluable. It is light, easy to use and does not deteriorate, and so much comes packaged in it these days that we never have a shortage.

WATERING

Watering can be a tricky subject. During Winter, containers still require moisture but *never* water if it is freezing or if frost threatens. Plants are better off being too dry than having their roots in an ice-block. Take particular care of window boxes which do not catch the rain because they are sheltered by the house. In Summer be prepared to water daily in the early morning or in the evening, but avoid watering when the sun might scorch the wet leaves. Be generous and do not make one watering can full of water stretch indefinitely. When the containers are brimming over with foliage and flowers the watering should be done at soil level – otherwise it will just run off the leaves onto the ground.

FEEDING

Plants grown in containers must be fed. Most of the Summer seasonal containers should be fed weekly or fortnightly. The perennial plantings on the whole need to be fed from April to September. The shrubs need weekly feeding: the hardy perennials less frequent feeds. We discuss feeding in more detail in the introduction to each section and in the recipes.

PEST CONTROL

You must control aphids, the nasty greenfly and blackfly that turn some summer annuals into a sticky mess. If you have just a few containers with astilbes or roses, lilies or hostas, for example, it is possible to simply pick off the aphids. As long as you do this every week you will be able to keep them under control. But if you have many soft-leafed plants, like petunias, and a lot of greenfly or blackfly, you will have to use chemicals to control them. For container gardens either aerosols or pellets seem to be the best method. The advantage of aerosols is that you can use as much or as little as you like and then put the top on – and use again the next time you see aphids.

The recent introduction of combined feed and insecticide pellets for pushing into the soil around the roots is a useful development and appears to work very successfully. They cannot be used with all plants so do read the instructions carefully – as you should before using any of these preparations.

It is possible to buy insecticides which you dilute and either spray or water over your plants. Although these are more economical than aerosols you will find the instructions given are for making large quantities which are difficult to scale down. You would be hard pressed to use even four litres (half a gallon) of insecticide in a whole patio garden – let alone for a few containers. And the excess should *never* be put down the drain. Do not use these products unless you have a garden and a safe place to dispose of the excess solution. There is an insecticide on the market called Abol-G which comes in crystal form in pint-sized sachets. If you are able to use a pint this is a good choice because it does not harm bees.

CLIMATE

Climate makes a great difference to container gardening and will affect the times of flowering and planting. In Scotland, and the north of England the Summer season is several weeks shorter than in the south-west.

All our perennial plants, shrubs and Winter and Spring displays were growing in London during the bad Winter of '85/86.

Though we did not have a greenhouse some of our plants were protected and this is referred to in the appropriate recipe, although the majority were left to fend for themselves. Some plants in particular recipes suffered noticeably. The white narcissi were stunted by the freeze and the ivies were devastated by the cruel winds which came after the thaw. However, we have still included these in the recipes because the Winter was so exceptional.

Other Winters have been different – in '82/83 cyclamens survived outside in London window boxes right through to the Spring. So let's try more of them please although we could not confidently recommend their use outside the south-east.

PERENNIAL RECIPES

INTRODUCTION TO THE PERENNIAL RECIPES

Although traditionally only annuals and perhaps a few conifers and camellias have been used as permanent features in containers, there are lots of other plants that can be grown. Some dwarf shrubs are ideally suited to container growing and others will let themselves be confined for a few years. Permanent groupings can be more unusual and rewarding to look after too.

Of course there will always be difficult decisions. The first you come up against is whether to fill your container up with two or three smallish plants, only to find that they have grown so much by the end of the first season that one of the plants just has to go. Or should you watch a single plant and try and convince yourselves and your friends that your true interest is in the art of understatement and Japanese style gardening? Each recipe suggests the number of plants to buy with this problem in mind.

Naturally we try to avoid bare earth and often the only way to do this – especially if your centre piece grows quite slowly – is to surround it with varieties that are rampant. In a garden these would be written off as invasive. However, things are much easier to control in a tub than a garden, and invasive plants have an important role. For example in Recipe 30 we have used *Sedum reflexum* as a short-term filler while the conifers and heathers become well established. As soon as it has served its purpose, pull it out.

Another problem is maintaining the plants in good condition. Growing things in containers is a little like framing pictures: the viewer expects something special. So if your plants have been exposed to a biting cold north-east wind, and even your hardy old Ilex is feeling sorry for itself, they will hardly grace your container. The easiest way to prevent shrubs suffering wind-burn and cold is to move them. Shrubs have a greatly increased chance of survival against a south or south-west facing wall.

If you cannot move them, fix a shelter against the north and north-easterly wind. Sheets of clear plastic a few millimetres thick are available at builders merchants. A more rustic alternative is wattle fencing. This can be quite difficult to get hold of in cities such as London but will be found with greater ease in the country, in East Anglia, for example.

Where the shrub being grown is less than fully hardy and temperatures are sinking, we have found polythene bubble gives effective protection. If the plant in question is a Coprosma as in Recipe 27, either wrap the polythene bubble around the whole trough or make a wigwam shape over the tub, stapling it down the side. This method saved sure fatalities in the winter of '85/86. Do not forget to remove the cover as soon as the weather improves and to water the plants – otherwise they could die of dehydration.

Because hardy perennials die back underground each year the new growth which emerges each Spring is fresh and green and unspoilt by Winter weather. This makes them particularly suitable for growing in containers. Alas, the new growth is very tasty to slugs and, to a lesser extent, aphids. Slugs are easy to control in containers because you can see them making their ascent. Be brave and pull them off! If you would rather use a preventative approach, surround the container with slug pellets and put a few on the soil. However, it's best to avoid using these if you have pets or small children. If you prefer not to use pellets, water with an anti-slug solution. Aphids are a problem you are bound to encounter, especially if you are growing roses. If you have only a few plants, why not just pick off the blackfly or greenfly or whatever? This is certainly possible with roses as they have a nice hard stem. If you have a small tub or hanging basket try the combined feed and insecticide pellets. If you have larger, more mature plants that require spraying use an aerosol unless you can use a pint of insecticide at a time.

Although perennials alone are a delight, they do make for dull empty containers during Winter and Spring. To compensate for this we have underplanted spring bulbs wherever possible.

Another factor which will influence how good your plants look is the soil you are using and your feeding policy. Hardy perennials, especially if they are tall growers, should be fed only monthly – otherwise they become leggy. But shrubs need to be fed every week from late April to September. There are lots of feeds on the market and none of them will do any harm although some might suit you better than others because of the way they are dispensed. We use Phostrogen, Liquinure and Chempack a lot, and find Chempack especially useful because it comes in crystal form. Chempak's Number 4 feed is the best general purpose mixture. They recommend Number 2, which helps root growth in the early season and Number 4, which has a higher potash content and encourages flowering mid-to-late season.

Then we come to soil. Use a John Innes No 2 or 3 or Fisons Greenleaf if you are growing shrubs. Another alternative is Chempak Potting Base. One of the active ingredients of compost is nitrogen and this starts to be dispersed when it reacts with water. So if you buy a peat-based soil that has been damp and stored for some time it may have lost all its nitrogen. The advantage of using Chempak – which comes in a dry pack that you mix with peat – is that your soil is fresh, active and ready to go as soon as you water, though do plan what you are going to mix it in. Once you have got the plant established the problem is maintaining the structure of the soil – soil tends to compact and lose its texture in containers. This is particularly noticeable if you have a poor batch of John Innes. It is not easy to fork in organic matter as you might in a garden because the roots, unable to go deep, tend to criss cross the whole pot. You should therefore take away as much of the top soil as you can each March, and then replace the top soil with new soil and wet peat. If you are only able to remove 2½cm (1″) of soil, then replace only with wet peat. If you are able to remove 10–12½cm (4–5″) of soil, replace with 7½cm (3″) of new soil and 2½–5cm (1–2″) of wet peat. The peat should be wetted first, otherwise it will absorb water and prevent the water from reaching the roots. Small bales of peat are now available in Woolworths and these are very useful for the container gardener.

Another question that often presents difficulties is where and when to buy plants.

Shrubs are best bought and planted in March. Choose them yourself from a good garden centre where you can see their shape, size and branch formation. Hardy perennials can be planted in October or through the Winter until April as long as the soil is not frozen. However, you may not be able to buy the plants you want in garden centres in October. They do tend to limit stocks at this time of the year because the unsold plants are vulnerable to frost damage in their little plastic pots. Unfortunately, if you have waited till October to buy your plants it is already quite late to order plants from a mail order catalogue. But not too late – so do not postpone it. Mail order catalogues are available in September and this is when keen gardeners place their orders. The drawback of mail ordering is that they have a minimum charge, so that although on

the whole plants purchased by mail order are cheaper than garden centre plants the minimum charge might well cancel this out.

If you wait until April to buy your plants the garden centres will have a much larger stock of hardy perennials. The drawback – and there has to be one – is that now you've missed the chance to underplant your summer flowering perennials with spring flowering bulbs.

In the following recipes which include hardy perennials, shrubs and alpines you will find that very many of the perennials have to be divided every second or third year. We have therefore included in this introduction a section on 'Dividing' for you to refer back to. Several of the shrubs will also need pruning and trimming – so following 'Dividing' is 'Pruning'.

Not all of the shrubs we have used can be pruned and kept 'contained'. Some will have to be periodically repotted into larger containers and eventually consigned to a garden.

Not all hardy perennials can be divided. Some are best discarded after two years and replaced. Each recipe tells you what to do. If you want to plant a container and leave it – read on. If you want to try a seasonal planting and have lots of changes then turn to the second and larger section of the book. If you have more than one container you will probably want some seasonal colour and a taste of something more permanent.

DIVIDING

This is really a very simple task and nothing to be afraid of. Choose an Autumn day (if we are having an Indian Summer postpone the dividing until the weather is a little cooler) and arm yourself with the following.

Newspaper (if the operation has to be done on the kitchen floor).
Rubber gloves.
A sharp knife.
A basin of water and things like cloths and dustpans, etc.
A bag for rubbish.

Knock the box or container as best you can against or with something wooden in order to loosen the rootball.

Turn the pot onto its side and pull the rootball out. Then try to split up the different plant groups. Just pull them apart – roots attached of course. Put the different varieties in groups. Then take the crown of the plant you want to split: it will have a rather tired centre and the leaves will probably be holed from insects, and dark and fibrous. Around this will be smaller, fresher, newer plantlets. All you have to do is to pull away these plantlets – and their roots – from the parent plant. In gardening books this operation is usually illustrated showing two garden forks placed back to back forcing the crown and the new plants apart. You should be able to do it with your hands.

Put the plantlets into the basin of water while you sort out the rest of the subjects. The old crown is best thrown away. Refill your container in the same way as you did initially and replant the new material. You will need some new soil – ideally you should renew all the soil. If you live in a big city the soil quality of top few inches will be spoilt by pollution and you are after all going to some trouble to remake the container. You will not have another opportunity to empty it for two or three years.

If you feel reluctant to renew the soil, at least make good the shortfall of soil (there always is one) with new soil and put a layer of wet peat on the surface.

When emptying containers you will find that ivies in particular are very greedy for root room and can be difficult to get out. We try not to use too much ivy for this reason. If you have a shrub or an ivy which has grown too big, unpack the box in the way we have just described.

Split the ivies by pulling them apart, and trim their roots by at least a third. This will not hinder their growth. Now replant the most attractive stems.

With a shrub that has been in a container more than three or four years the first thing to do is look at its shape and ask yourself whether it is worth keeping. If the shrub needs a light trimming just follow the instructions in the recipe; if it is massively too big it will need to be pruned.

PRUNING

In several recipes you will need to prune either shrubs or roses. Many people are timid about pruning but there is nothing to be apprehensive about – if you are cutting back a healthy plant at the right time of the year it is very difficult to cause any permanent damage – unless you decimate it!

For container gardening you have to be particularly conscious of shape: You will need to prune the plant into the shape that suits your container. Cut back shrubs at the time shown in the individual recipes. This is important because if you cut them back at the wrong end of the season you may cut off the very stems on which the plant will be making its new flowers.

Shrubs can be shortened because they are becoming too large; because they are scantly leafed and naked looking around their base (taking out the top growth will encourage them to shoot from the lower buds); or because they seem to be losing their vigour. They should also be thinned out when the branches start to cross each other. Shoots that die after the Winter should be cut back to healthy stems or back to ground level if they come from the base.

Roses too need to be pruned when they are getting too big. Cut back roses in early March or a little later if the weather is very cold. You should be aiming to have them pruned just as the sap is starting to rise and Spring growth is beginning. If you prune too early you will leave the bush you hope to take through the Summer vulnerable to frost damage and if you prune too late you will be cutting off the plant's new growth.

Cut the stems with sharp secateurs above an outward facing bud and slope the cut so that it backs up to the bud. This stops water running off the new cut onto the new bud. New growth will break out from this bud so choose one that will give you stems at the right height from soil level. Again be prepared to cut off any dead wood or thin out any crossing stems.

Most of the small patio roses which we have used in the book will need tidying up after the Winter. Cut off the stems that have been caught by the frost, then thin out crossing wood and trim any wayward stems. Although the principles of rose pruning should be remembered, these roses do not require the thorough pruning given to garden roses.

We have mentioned plants losing their 'vigour' without expanding on it. If a plant is looking jaded you can do a number of things. You can review your own care (do you water it and feed it regularly?); you can put it into new soil or you can trim it back. If you are opting for a trim then do repot the plant into new soil as well. After all, you want new roots to grow quickly so give them clean, aerated, wholesome soil.

If you change the soil this will also give you a chance to do some root-pruning. Although gardeners have no need to root-prune it is often essential that container gardeners do. The roses in our hanging basket recipe were root-pruned simply to fit in the basket! Root-pruning should be carried out in March. Never remove more than a third of the root and replant quickly into a new pot with new soil, some bonemeal and peat. Afterwards water daily for two weeks. Most shrubs can also be root-pruned.

MISCELLANEOUS BOXES, TROUGHS, TUBS AND BARRELS

1 LAZY TUB

This combination of Spring, Summer, late Summer and Winter flowering plants gives year-round interest.

Site
Sun or partial shade; during Winter, the pot requires protection from east and north-easterly winds.

Container
Tub: 40cm (16″) in diameter, 35cm (14″) high.

Plant
Be prepared to plant in October. Order plants in September although all of these should be available at a garden centre.

Ingredients
  1 Hebe 'Bowles' Variety.
  2 *Liriope muscari*.
  1 Periwinkle *Vinca major* 'Elegantissima'.
  1 *Geranium* x *riversleianum* 'Russell Prichard'.
25 litres of John Innes No 3 or a peat-based compost.
Sufficient drainage material to cover the base of the pot to a depth of 2½cm (1″).

Method
1. Soak all the plants in a basin of water.
2. Put drainage material together with about 12½cm (5″) of soil in the bottom of the container.
3. Position the hebe against the front edge of the pot with the vinca beside it. Place the liriope to the centre left and the geranium towards the back and the right.
4. Fill the pot with the rest of the soil.

5. Ensure the neck of the plants (the point where the stem goes into the soil) is level with the new soil and is 2½cm (1″) below the rim of the pot.
6. Water thoroughly with at least 2 litres (3½ pints) of water and then fill in any holes in the soil.

Aftercare
Keep the container moist during Winter and water regularly during the Summer. Feed every three weeks from mid May onwards.

   Cut off the flower spikes of the liriope right down to the ground after flowering. Be prepared to divide the geranium and the liriope after the second year (see page 7).

2 TWELVE MONTHS OF FOLIAGE

This pretty combination of small shrubs will become increasingly lovely as the plants mature, interweave and blend with the terracotta window-box.

Site
Window ledge in full sun or partial shade.

Container
Large terracotta window box: 80cm (32″) long, 20cm (8″) wide, 19cm (7½″) deep.

Plant
Either in October when the arrangement can be filled out with primroses or in May when the nicotiana can be planted out.

Looks its best
Good all year round – the high spots depend on what you add.

Ingredients
1 *Euonymus fortunei radicans* 'Silver Queen'.
1 *Pittosporum tenuifolium* 'Variegatum'.
1 *Hebe* 'Bowles Variety'.
1 *Hedera helix* 'Adam'.
    Either 3 *Primula vulgaris* (primroses) planted for the Autumn *or* 3 *Nicotiana alata* 'Lime Green' (tobacco plants) planted for May.
25 litres of John Innes No 3 or a peat-based compost.
Sufficient drainage material to cover the base of the window box to a depth of 1–2cm (½–¾″).

Method
1. Soak all the plants in a saucer of water for at least ten minutes.
2. Put the drainage material on the base of the container. Put a third of the soil into the container.
3. Position the hebe in the centre left or right and the ivy right against the front edge to balance it up on the side left empty. The euonymus should go behind the ivy. The pittosporum should be positioned in the centre and middle of the box.
4. *If May planting* Position the nicotiana in suitable gaps and add the rest of the soil.
    If Autumn planting Add another third of the soil and arrange the primroses around the shrubs. Top up with the remaining soil.
5. Now water thoroughly. There are bound to be some gaps in the soil level which will need filling in after watering. Make sure that the soil is packed down in each corner.
6. *If you have Spring planted* When the nicotiana are over, just pull them out gently. You can then plant primroses in their place.
    If you have Autumn planted The primroses will be showing plenty of leaf and, if you are lucky, some flower as well the following Spring. Pull them out of the box with a handfork and either plant them in a garden or put them into a small flower pot where they will happily grow throughout the Summer as long as you keep them watered. Then, when the risk of frost is over, plant the nicotiana.
    Those same primroses can be planted again the following Autumn. Divide them before planting (see page 7). You will almost certainly have too many now for this one box.

Aftercare
Keep the soil moist through Winter and Summer but remember not to water before frosty weather. Feed weekly from May to September.

Nicotiana are a tasty treat for blackfly and greenfly: be prepared to spray weekly throughout the Summer (see page 3).

Trim the euonymus back and thin it out in February to keep it in shape. Pick out the growing tips of pittosporum in February to encourage bushy growth. This shrub can get quite big so be prepared to cut it back in February in the same way that you would shear a hedge.

The ivy is less rampant than many but could still take over the box: if after two or three years you find this happening empty out the box and split the ivy.

3 SOLITUDE

This solo plant is given a place here simply because although not often grown in containers, it is handsome and simple.

Site
Sun or shade.

Container
Large bowl or barrel. This one is 50cm (20″) in diameter, 35cm (14″) deep.

Plant
Late April, early May. Make sure your garden centre will have the plant in and if necessary order in March.

Looks its best
Looks more golden-leafed in Summer but otherwise the same all the year round.

Ingredients
1 Japanese holly *Ilex crenata* 'Golden Gem'.
60 litres of John Innes No 3. Sufficient drainage material to cover the base of the container to a depth of 5cm (2″).

Method
1. Soak the plant in a basin of water for at least 20 minutes before planting.
2. If the container is heavy, place it in the position you want to keep it in before you fill it with soil.
3. Put the drainage material followed by a third of the soil into the container.
4. Position the plant nicely in the middle and put the rest of the soil around the sides.
5. Water thoroughly with at least 2 litres (3½ pints) of water and then fill in any gaps that might appear in the soil.

Aftercare
Keep the plant well watered and feed weekly with a liquid feed like Liquinure, Phostrogen or Chempak 3 from May till September.

In March of the second year, remove the top 2½cm (1″) of soil and replace it with peat or shredded wood bark.

4 SOLID AND VERY IMPRESSIVE IN SPRING

In prominent positions conifers have a very solid feel about them. In this recipe the pieris is delightful from April onwards when the new red foliage appears. By July it has turned a dark glossy green but in between times it is a brilliant shade of lime green.

Site
Sun or Shade.

Container
Barrel 55cm (22″) in diameter, 40cm (16″) deep.

Plant
Early October and May for additional summer colour.

Looks its best
April/May.

Ingredients
1 *Pieris formosa.*
1 *Thuja occidentalis* 'Smaragd'.
2 *Juniperus horizontalis* 'Glauca'.
2 *Hedera helix* 'Goldchild'.
6 white *Narcissus triandrus* 'Thalia'.
75 litres of peat-based compost: as these plants are likely to come in large pots we have allowed less soil than you would expect to use.
Sufficient drainage material to cover the base to a depth of 5cm (2″).

Method
1. Soak all the plants in a basin of water before planting.
2. Ensure your barrel has holes drilled in the bottom. Put it in the position where it is to stand – it will be very heavy when it is filled with soil. Then place 5cm (2″) of drainage material in the bottom.
3. Add soil, leaving enough space to accommodate the largest plant pot. Plant the largest first, add more soil, then plant the next largest and so on.
4. The junipers are best placed at the very edges of the barrel where they can trail over the edge. If you intend to put this display in an exposed position put the conifer on the windy side to give protection to the pieris.
5. Add one ivy in between the junipers, and the other besides the pieris.
6. Plant the bulbs in clumps 5–6cm (2–2½″) deep.
7. Fill the container to within 2½cm (1″) of the top with soil.

8. Water thoroughly with four litres (7 pints) of water and top up with soil if any gaps have emerged.
9. After the dying daffodils have started to turn yellow the display starts to look very untidy. Cut off the dead daffodil stems and, gently so as not to harm the bulbs or cause too much root disturbance, make a 10cm (4″) deep, 7½cm (3″) wide hole in the soil. If you can do this – and you should be able to – buy a nice bright red upright pelargonium such as 'Ringo' and pop it into the space. The best time to do this is May.

Aftercare
Keep the barrel well watered and begin feeding the plants in May. A weekly general purpose feed should be given until early September.

In the March of the barrel's second year remove the top centimetres or inch or two of soil and replace it with new soil, or with the old soil together with half a bucket of peat.

This combination should last for many years. All the plant ingredients are slow growers.

5 SCENTED HUES OF PINK AND BLUE

A background of interesting foliage and pretty perennials provides the backdrop for the heavily scented Brompton stocks. Despite the frail appearance of the silver-leaved plants, they all survive the Winter above ground, giving you just a hint of what's to come.

Site
A window ledge with at least four hours sun a day.

Container
Home-made wooden box: 75cm (30″) long, 18½cm (7½″) wide, 17½cm (7″) deep.

Plant
Late September/early October when strips of Brompton stocks become available.

Looks its best
Most showy when the stocks are in flower. The dianthus which follow two to three weeks later are delightful but much smaller.

Ingredients
1 strip of Brompton stocks *Matthiola incana*. We have used an ordinary Brompton stock, mixed colours, which give a mixture of double and single flowered varieties in delicate shades of pink, mauve and cream. These are bi-annuals.
1 strip or 4 plants of dianthus *Dianthus* 'Alpine', at least 15cm (6″) tall. Alternatively use 'Mrs Sinkins' (white) or 'Excelsior' (deep pink).
3 small cotton lavender *Santolina chamaecyparissus or* 2 cotton lavenders and one *Santolina virens* which has rich green foliage as opposed to silver foliage.
2 *Phlox subulata* 'White Delight'.
1 Variegated ivy *Hedera helix* 'Goldchild'.
1 Common ivy *Hedera helix* (optional).
25 litres of John Innes No 2 or a peat-based compost.

Method
1. Soak all the plants in a basin of water for at least ten minutes.
2. Put about 1cm (½″) of drainage material in the bottom of the box plus one third of the soil.
3. Plant the santolina first. Add more soil and plant the phlox. These should go right at the front of the box where they will trail over. If you are using ivy, plant it at this stage.
4. Add most of the remaining soil, keeping back about half a bucket for topping up.
5. Knock the stocks and dianthus out of their strips and pull the plantlets apart. Dig holes for the roots with your finger and drop the plants in, firming the soil around each one.
6. Water thoroughly with 4 litres (1 gallon) of water in a watering can with a rose.
7. Top up with soil. Be particularly careful that the corners are properly filled and are not acting as gulleys taking the water right through to the window ledge.

Aftercare
Keep the soil moist throughout the winter. Begin feeding early – in March – with fortnightly feeds.

Trim the santolina in April to the shape you want. You can reduce it by a third of its size.

Deadhead the stocks as they finish flowering. When they have all finished flowering either remove the plants – which is difficult without disturbing the other plants – or cut them off at their base.

If you want to have the same display again you will have to empty this box and replant more stocks in the Autumn. Make sure when you do empty the container that you manage to remove all the old stock roots. Alternatively, replace the stocks with another popular biennial, *Cheiranthus* 'Tom Thumb Mixed' or 'Golden Bedder'.

The flowering stems of the dianthus should be cut to ground level after the first frost. Although these plants can be left in the box year after year they are best replaced with new plants every two years.

If the ivy has become very large, separate out the good young shoots which have their roots attached and discard the woodier older stems.

6 MINIMALIST STYLE

Though the flowering period of this elegant dwarf evergreen rhododendron is short, its shape justifies its permanent inclusion in this rather superior type of container.

Site
Partial shade, sheltered from north-easterly winds.

Container
Olive jar or similar. This one is 50cm (20″) high 37½cm (15″) in diameter at its widest point.

Plant
Spring or Autumn.

Looks its best
May.

Ingredients
1 dwarf evergreen rhododendron *Rhododendron* 'Scarlet Wonder'; when buying, do check the size and make sure you are buying an evergreen.
1 *Aubrieta deltoidea* 'Dr Mules'.
35 litres of ericaceous soil or Fisons Greenleaf.
Pieces of polystyrene as drainage material.

Method
1. Soak the rhododendron in a basin of water for 20 minutes.
2. Put the drainage material in the bottom one third of the container. Break up the polystyrene as much as you can if the pieces are large; for preference use the pearl-sized beads.
3. Add one third of the soil. If you are using chunks of polystyrene shake the container so that the soil falls down into the air spaces.
4. If the container in which you bought the rhododendron is larger than the neck of the olive jar remove it from the pot and gently swish the root ball in water. Try not to remove too much soil – just enough to get the roots comfortably through the neck of the jar. Then spread the roots out in the soil inside the jar and put the remainder of the soil on top. Plant the aubrieta simply by making a hole in the soil with your fingers. Keep the soil level about 1cm (½″) from the rim of the pot – otherwise your aubrieta will have difficulty scrambling over.
5. Water thoroughly with two litres (half a gallon) of water applied slowly and then top up any holes that appear in the soil level.

Aftercare
Be careful about positioning. This plant prefers partial shade and dappled sun – glaring hot exposures should be avoided.

Never let the plant dry out. This is definitely a plant you should stand in a saucer because without Summer moisture it will not flower the following year. Feed the plant with Phostrogen or Chempak 8 during the Summer.

7 BRIDAL WREATH

This fairytale arc of white flower is aptly named bridal wreath. It graces a fairly shaded basement, hence the strange angle of the photograph. Can you just see the geranium planted below? – ready to take over the torch and keep this display interesting throughout the Summer.

Site
Sheltered with a little sun.

Container
Large urn or barrel. Urn: 80cm (32″) high, 62½cm (25″) in diameter at its widest point.
Barrel: some barrels are a little shallow for this planting. Try to find one with a minimum depth of 40cm (16″) and a diameter of 55cm (22″).

Plant
Late March/early May.

Looks its best
May.

Ingredients
　1　bridal wreath *Spiraea* x *arguta*.
　2　*Geranium* x *riversleianum* 'Russell Prichard'.
For barrel size given:
　75　litres of soil.
For urn size given:
100　litres of soil. (John Innes No 3 or peat-based compost.)

Method
1.　Soak the plants in a basin for 20 minutes.
2.　Put the drainage material in the bottom of the container. Use 2½cm (1″) for the barrel and 7½cm (3″) for the urn.
3.　Put two-thirds of the soil into the container together with a good big handful of bonemeal.
4.　*FOR AN URN* Remove the spiraea from its pot. The rootball may be too large to fit into the top of the urn, so wash the roots very gently. Remove no more soil than is absolutely necessary. Spread

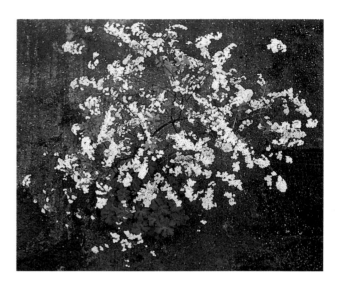

the roots over the soil in the pot and cover with half the remaining soil. Now plant the geraniums which may also need to have their roots washed. Fill the container with soil to within 2½cm (1″) of the rim. Water slowly with 2 litres (3½ pints) of water and fill in any dimples that might appear in the soil level.

　FOR A BARREL Add half the soil. Tease out the roots of the spiraea from its rootball to encourage it to anchor itself and spread into its new home. Fill in the space around the spiraea rootball with soil. Plant the geraniums at the angles of 4 o'clock and 8 o'clock on either side of the spiraea. Water thoroughly and then top up any holes that might appear in the soil level with soil or peat.

Aftercare
Keep the plants moist. Each Spring take off the top 5cm (2″) of soil. Either re-use the old soil, adding half a bucket of peat, or replace this top layer of soil with new soil. It is important to incorporate peat to prevent the soil compacting.

　If you want to trim the spiraea, shorten the stems after the plant has flowered. To tidy the geranium, cut all the stems and leaves back to ground level in November. The geranium will need to be divided every two or three years (see page 7).

8 AN OPENING FOR A BLUEBELL

Bluebells are usually thought of as wild flowers – as indeed they are – but they can be bought from bulb specialists. This simple combination will grace any shady, damp spots.

Site
Shade or partial shade, and shelter.

Container
Medium terracotta pot: 30cm (12″) in diameter, 32½cm (13″) deep.

Plant
October.

Looks its best
April.

Method
1. Soak the plants in a basin of water.
2. Put the drainage material in the bottom of the pot.
3. Add half the soil.
4. Position the hosta and fern at the back of the pot and put ten bluebell bulbs in a clump at the front.

Ingredients
10 bluebells *Hyacinthoides non-scripta (Scilla nutans)*. (Order these from specialist bulb nurseries in September.)
 1 *Polystichum setiferum* 'Acutilobum'.
 1 *Hosta* 'Thomas Hogg'.
25 litres of John Innes No 2 soil or Levingtons Multi-purpose compost.
 2 or 3 handfuls of horticultural grit, gravel or small pieces of polystyrene for drainage.

Aftercare
Water regularly and keep the soil moist. If you find it difficult to keep the soil sufficiently moist place the pot on a saucer which will help.

During the growing season from April to September feed the pot monthly with a general liquid feed such as Phostrogen.

The hosta will come to dominate this pot and after two years should be divided (see page 7).

9 DARK, RICH, INTRICATE AND GREEN

This moist looking concoction of ferns and hostas will tolerate the shadiest of places and give year-round interest.

Site
Partial or even full shade.

Container
This particular display is planted in a 'Grosfillex' plastic trough with a specially designed reservoir underneath. This allows the plant to take what water it requires – and when it requires. Grosfillex is a manufacturers name. These troughs are widely available although this actual model is no longer made. Although this kind of trough is very useful for those away a lot, any ordinary box will do just as well. This box is 87½cm (35″) long, 32½cm (13″) wide and 27½cm (11″) deep.

Plant
Late September/early October.

Looks its best
May to end July.

Method
1. Soak all the plants in a basin of water.
2. Put the drainage material in the bottom half of the trough.
3. Now position all the plants. The hostas should be centre, right and left. The ferns should be in the centre of their section of the box – not hard against the edge, as they form the centre of the display in the Winter. The ajuga and the bergenia should be placed along and close to the front edge of the box.
4. Now fill up the box with the rest of the soil. Make sure that the soil level is 2½cm (1″) below the rim of the pot – no more or less.
5. Water thoroughly with a watering can with a rose, using at least 2 litres (3½ pints) of water.
6. Check that there are no gaps in the soil level and be particularly careful that corners are properly filled with soil.

Ingredients
2 *Polystichum setiferum* 'Acutilobum'.
1 Hart's tongue fern *Asplenium scolopendrium*.
2 *Aquilegia vulgaris* 'Atrata'.
2 *Hosta ventricosa* 'Variegata'.
2 *Bergenia cordifolia*.
2 *Ajuga reptans* 'Atropurpurea'.
70 litres of peat-based compost or John Innes No 2 soil.
1 bucketful of very small pieces of polystyrene.

Aftercare
Be particularly careful to ensure that this container does not dry out. The drawback of using a home-made wooden box is that you will not be able to find trays to fit underneath it, but you can reduce the risk of it drying out by making sure that it is placed in a sheltered and shady place.

Feed this container once a month during the growing season from April to September.

The hostas will need dividing in the second year (see page 7).

10 BLEEDING HEARTS AND WHITE LILIES

This little pot is given a very fragile look by the dicentra.

Site
Shady and sheltered position, which you can get to easily for watering.

Container
Small round pot: 25cm (10″) in diameter, 30cm (12″) deep and a saucer to fit.

Plant
March: the zantedeschia has to be planted separately in March and started into growth on a window sill. Order the zantedeschia from one of the bulb specialists listed in the back of the book in February.

Looks its best
From late April to July.

Ingredients
  1 *Dicentra eximia*.
  1 *Sedum sieboldii* 'Mediovariegatum'.
  1 *Zantedeschia aethiopica* 'Crowborough'.
12 litres of John Innes No 2 or a peat-based compost.
  1 15cm (4″) pot.
Horticultural grit or broken crocks for drainage.

Method
1. In January order the zantedeschia from a bulb specialist. When you receive the rhizome store it in a cool place until you are ready to plant it. In March plant it in a 15cm (4″) pot using John Innes No 2 soil or a multi-purpose compost. Stand the planted up pot in a dish of water for ten minutes after planting. Put it in a light but not too sunny window sill. Water sparingly until growth starts to show. Then keep it very moist.
2. In late April assemble the other plants. The sedum can be a difficult plant to buy: it is often considered tender and either not stocked at all or kept in the house plant section. It has survived two of the worst Winters of the century here without protection so we have continued to use it.

3. Soak the plants in a basin of water for at least ten minutes before planting.
4. Put 2½cm (1″) of drainage material into the container, followed by approximately 12½cm (5″) of soil. Now place the dicentra just off centre and place a 15cm (4″) pot beside it. Position the sedum hard against the edge of the container where the leaves can trail over the edge. Put the remaining soil around the two plants and the empty container. (If the sight of the empty container offends you turn it upside down and put a little soil over to mask it.)
5. Stand the pot in its saucer and water thoroughly.
6. When the risk of prolonged and severe frost is over replace the empty flower pot space with the zantedeschia.
7. Water thoroughly and fill in any holes in the soil that might have appeared with more soil or peat.

Aftercare
Water copiously from April to the end of July. The zantedeschia is often grown as a water margin plant so bear this in mind when you feel you may be over-watering. The dicentra will not mind generous watering. Water sparingly over Winter just keeping the soil moist, and begin watering the plants more generously in March when the weather permits.

Feed this container weekly from mid April until August. Over Winter put the pot in the most protected and sheltered position you can offer it. Wind can be almost as harmful as frost. Putting polythene bubble around it is the most effective means of protection but you must ensure there are a few holes in the polythene for ventilation. Do not dispose of the polythene until you are confident that you have had the last severe frost. The dicentra will need to be divided after the second year. Do this in November following the instructions for dividing given on page 7.

When dividing the dicentra you might well consider putting this arrangement into a larger tub. If you choose to do this add 20 or so *Narcissus cyclamineus* 'Tête-à-Tête'. These sweet little daffodils are delicately complimented by the feathery opening foliage of the dicentra.

11 FRILLY FUNNEL

Though less straightforward to plant than standard containers, chimneys are certainly worth planting up if you happen to have one. This display will tumble happily over the side of the chimney for a year or two but in the long term it will need a balustrade, balcony railing or fence to wind around.

Site
Sheltered, and with half a day's sun or more.

Container
Chimney pot. They come in varying sizes, ranging from 27½cm (11") to 40cm (16") in diameter. (They are all in effect too deep.)

Plant
Late September or early April.

Looks its best
May.

Ingredients
1 *Clematis macropetala*.
1 *Ajuga reptans* 'Burgundy Glow'.
20 litres of John Innes No 3.
A saucer big enough to sit the chimney in. This can be plastic or terracotta (Stewart Plastics make a square brown saucer which is very useful).
A circle of plastic sheeting, slightly larger than the diameter of the chimney.
A handful of bonemeal.
A large quantity of polystyrene or a few handfuls of gravel.

Method
1. Soak the plants for at least twenty minutes.
2. Put the chimney in the saucer in its intended resting place.
3. Measure 45cm (18") down from the top of the chimney and scratch a mark on the side.
4. Put broken polystyrene chunks about 2½cm (1") square into the container up to the level of the mark you have just made.
5. Make five or six holes in the piece of plastic and put this across the top of the polystyrene.
6. Now put approximately 2½cm (1") of drainage material on top of the plastic.
7. Add about two thirds of the soil and mix a handful of bonemeal with it.
8. Remove the clematis from the pot and just tease a few of the roots away from the rootball. Place it

in the chimney and now start to fill in the soil all round, remembering to leave a gap just to one side of the clematis for the ajuga.
9. Plant the ajuga as close as you can to the stems of the clematis.
   While it looks pretty cascading over the edge of the chimney it also protects the base stem of the clematis from the heat of the sun.

Aftercare
Water very regularly, especially during long dry periods. Feed fortnightly from the last fortnight in April until the end of September with a liquid feed.

It is important to get bushy growth well down at the base of the clematis. As it flowers on the stems made in the previous season you must cut it back immediately after flowering so as to let new stems grow in the Summer months. If you cut it back in Autumn you won't get any flowers the following year.

After flowering, cut out the flower bearing shoots. If the main stem is too long cut this back by one third. This may seem drastic – it is. You have to cut off all the leaf-bearing stems, leaving just some liana-type twine sticking out from your pot. But those buds along the stems will throw up new growth within days and the following year you will have a much bushier plant. Once you have a bushy plant let it romp.

12 COTONEASTER WITH A DIFFERENCE

This unusual plant is a quarter standard *Cotoneaster dammeri*. It has been berrying and flowering with little attention, but it berries much better if it is fed regularly – for three or four years. It will retain its manageable size with only the lightest trimming.

Site
Partial sun and shade; avoid very windy sites.

Container
White wooden box: 39cm (15½″) cube.

Plant
Late September.

Looks its best
June and January to March.

Ingredients
1 *quarter standard Cotoneaster dammeri* 'Coral Beauty'. (Order from a garden centre or specialist nursery.)
1 Christmas Rose *Helleborus niger*.
1 *Helleborus foetidus*.
1 *Hedera helix* 'Adam'.
1 *Viola x wittrockiana* 'Goldie'.
40 litres of John Innes No 3 or a peat-based compost.
A few crocks or some horticultural grit as drainage material.

Method
1. Soak all the plants in a basin of water for at least ten minutes.
2. Place the drainage material in the bottom of the tub.
3. Put half the soil into the tub together with a handful of bonemeal.
4. Take the cotoneaster first and, having removed it from the pot, just tease out a few of the roots to aid its establishment.
5. Place the hellebores to each side of the cotoneaster and the little pansy at the front. Trail the ivy over the front.
6. Now fill up the container with the rest of the soil and water thoroughly. If any holes appear, particularly down the side of the container, make sure that you fill them up.

Aftercare
Water regularly throughout the year. Give the cotoneaster monthly foliar feeds from April to September by spraying its leaves with the prescribed amount of dilute Phostrogen. Feed the whole container monthly from May to September. Aim to feed the cotoneaster fortnightly and the other plants monthly.

If the cotoneaster stems become too long, trim the stems in February. The hellebores will quickly spread and after the second year will have to be split up. Fork them out with a hand fork in late October/early November and then divide them as described on page 7.

13 ACER IN A ROUND POT

These lovely slow-growing trees are ideal for growing in pots. Just a little colour underneath is pretty but not essential.

Site
Part sun/part shade, protected from easterly and north-easterly winds.

Container:
Medium sized terracotta 'Cherub' pot: 30cm (12″) in diameter, 25cm (10″) deep.

Plant
Late September to early October if you want to use bulbs, otherwise late March.

Looks its best
This is delightful in early Spring.

Ingredients
  1 *Acer palmatum* 'Atropurpureum'.
  2 Maiden pinks *Dianthus deltoides* .
30 tulips *Tulipa tarda.*
12 litres of peat-based compost.
A small amount of horticultural grit, or small crumbs of polystyrene for drainage.

Method
1. Soak the acer in basin of water.
2. Put the drainage material in the base of the pot together with half of the soil.
3. Position the acer in the middle of the pot and fill in the gap around with soil to within 6¼cm (2½″). Now place the bulbs around the tree in a circle if an Autumn planting; if a Spring planting, position the dianthus against the edge of the pot to encourage it to fall over the side.

Aftercare
Water regularly and feed throughout the Spring and Summer months ie early May to September.

Let the bulbs die right back. Remove the seed pods from the bulbs as they appear. When the bulb foliage turns yellow and starts to look really untidy, cut it off.

Be prepared to repot this tree every two or three years if you want it to continue growing. If it has reached a size you are happy with there will be no need to go on repotting it but ensure you continue to feed it and renew the top 2½cm (1″) of soil each year.

14 A TALL SLIM FATSIA

This fatsia has had its problems with severe frost but it still continues to make a strong impact, the geums adding a strong colour contrast.

Site
Sunny sheltered position. In the Midlands and the North fatsias should only be grown against a sheltered wall.

Container
Small deep barrel: this one is painted with Rustin's Matt Black and is 35cm (14″) in diameter, 33½cm (13″) deep.

Plant
Late September to early October.

Looks its best
June.

Ingredients
 1 *Fatsia japonica.*
 3 *Geum chiloense* 'Mrs Bradshaw'.
20 red dwarf tulips *Tulipa greigii* 'Red Riding Hood'.
A small amount of polystyrene or gravel as drainage material.
35 litres of John Innes No 3 or a peat-based compost.

Optional
 2 feverfew *Chrysanthemum parthenium* 'Aureum': these should be added to the arrangement in May after the tulips are over.

Method
1. Soak all the plants in a basin of water for 20 minutes.
2. Place the drainage material in the bottom of the barrel.
3. Put two thirds of the soil into the barrel.
4. Position the fatsia and add more soil around its rootball. Now plant the geums.
5. The tulips should be planted in clumps at a depth of 7½cm (3″) in between the geums.
6. Top up with the rest of the soil making sure the neck of the plant 'floats' at the correct level of 2½cm (1″) below the rim of the pot.
7. Water thoroughly and fill in any holes that might appear in the soil level.

Aftercare
Water regularly and feed fortnightly.

Deadhead the tulips after flowering and cut yellowing foliage down to the ground in late May. The stems of the geums should be cut down to ground level after they have finished flowering in August/September.

These plants will have to be divided every second or third year. This is best done in March or April (see page 7).

The feverfew self-seed and if you want to keep them from year to year you will have to bring seedlings on in pots. Otherwise they will be unable to compete with the geums.

They certainly look attractive in Spring and early Summer and are so easy to grow it is worth trying to nurture a few. But, be warned, they do begin to look like daisies by July.

15 FOLIAGE IN WINTER AND SUMMER

This recipe is for an attractive mixture of variegated and coloured foliage. Surprisingly, most of the plants are evergreen so even in Winter it offers interest.

Site
Some hours of sun required.

Container
In this picture a Chinese glazed urn is used but any large tub or barrel would be suitable. This one is 55cm (22″) in diameter, 40cm (16″) deep.

Plant
April.

Looks its best
Late May/early June when the Iris flowers.

Ingredients
1 *Heuchera* 'Palace Purple'. (Mail order the following three Jan/Feb or buy from a garden centre in April.)
1 *Hosta* 'Thomas Hogg'.
1 *Iris pallida* 'Variegata'.
1 *Tolmiea menziesii.* Available in garden centres in April/May and in chain stores where it is sold as a houseplant.
60 litres of John Innes No 2 or a peat-based compost
Cubes of polystyrene (which are usefully light) to cover the bottom of the container to a depth of 2½cm (1″).

Method
1. Soak all the plants in a basin of water for 20 minutes.
2. Place the drainage material in the bottom of the container together with half the soil.
3. Arrange the plants in the container. Place the heuchera to the back and the tolmiea to the front so that it can cascade over the rim. Try not to crowd the iris. Position it and the hosta to the left and right centre of the pot.
4. Fill the container with the remaining soil and water thoroughly.
5. Carefully fill up any gaps that appear after watering, especially those in between the plants.

Aftercare
Keep the soil moist and feed monthly with a liquid feed from April until September.

This recipe provides a gourmet treat for slugs so keep a watchful eye out for holes in the leaves and slimy trails. If you discover slugs, water the leaves with a prepared solution of slug killer.

The heuchera and hosta will need to be divided after two years (see page 7). The iris will form new bulbs which will easily divide: divide them every two to three years and replant the largest of the new bulbs. The smaller bulbs will flower in subsequent years but will have to be allowed a little more time to mature.

The tolmiea will make new plantlets in the tub. Roots will grow from leaves where they touch the soil. Little plantlets grow on the stems as well and although these are not rooted they are very easy to root if you detach them and put them in moist compost.

These plantlets can be planted outside or taken inside as a houseplant. It is useful to bring on a new tolmeia against the day when the original one will get fibrous and shabby looking.

16 A BALANCED FLUE

This simple combination of three shrubs is symmetrically pleasing and subtly coloured.

Site
Needs half a day's sun and shelter from north and north-easterly winds. In areas outside the south and west of England grow against a south-facing wall.

Container
Chimney pot. These come in varying sizes with diameters from 27½cm (11″) to 40cm (16″). They are all really too deep and will need to have filling material in their base.

Looks its best
May to October. Pictured in May but hypericum has yellow flowers in July and August.

Ingredients
1 *Weigela florida* 'Foliis Purpureis'.
1 *Hypericum* x *moserianum* 'Tricolor'.
1 *Jasminum officinale*.
20 litres of John Innes No 3 soil.
A large amount of polystyrene – enough to fill the lower half of the chimney.
A circular piece of thick polythene, larger than the diameter of the chimney.
A saucer for chimney to stand on.
A handful of bonemeal.

Method
1. Soak all the plants in a basin of water.
2. Prepare the chimney for planting by following steps 2–7 in the Method section of Recipe 11 (Frilly Funnel) on page 20.
3. If the shrubs are in 20cm (8″) pots, you will need to gently wash the rootball and remove just enough soil to be able to fit the plant into the chimney. Put all three plants into the chimney at the same time and be very careful to fill around the roots with soil as you go and not to leave any airspaces. Remember too that the neck of the plants – the point where the stem emerges from the soil – should be buried to the same depth in its new home as it was in its old. Keep the soil level 2½cm (1″) below the chimney rim in order to provide a catchment area for water.
4. Water thoroughly and fill any gaps that appear in the surface with more soil.

Aftercare
Keep the plants moist and feed weekly from May to September. When watering take care to water the soil and make sure the plants are really getting wetted.

The weigela should be trimmed after flowering if necessary. Cut out the oldest shoots first. The hypericum can be trimmed back to within 7½cm (3″) or 10cm (4″) of the soil level in March to encourage it to bush. Do not trim it if you want it to grow long trails.

The jasmine does not take too kindly to being cut back so be prepared to place the chimney against a railing or a wall where the jasmine can romp away. Within three or four years the roots of these plants will take up almost the whole width of the chimney. If you want to empty it you have the advantage of being able to push them out from underneath as well as pull them out from the top. There is of course no need to empty the pot and if you continue feeding and topping up with peat every year the plants can survive for many years.

17 PLAIN HOSTAS WITH SPRING BULBS

This simple pot of hostas highlights all the joys of growing perennials. Watching the plant emerge from the soil each year is as satisfying as watching a sunset. Underplant with bulbs to get double value from your pot.

Site
Partial to full shade.

Container
Medium terracotta pot with saucer: 40cm (16″) in diameter, 35cm (14″) high.

Plant
October. Order the plants from a garden centre or mail order catalogue in September.

Looks its best
May and June.

Ingredients
 3 *Hosta* 'Thomas Hogg'.
20 Striped squills *Puschkinia scilloides.*
15 litres of John Innes No 2 or peat-based compost.
Gravel or a small amount of fine polystyrene as drainage material.

Method
1. Soak the hostas in a basin of water for at least 20 minutes.
2. Put the drainage material in the bottom of the container.
3. Put two thirds of the soil in the container.
4. Position the plants and put the rest of the soil around them.
5. The puschkinias are very small bulbs. Plant them about 2½cm (1″) below the soil surface.
6. Cover the soil and water thoroughly, topping up the soil level if it has settled.

Aftercare
Water regularly and feed monthly with liquid feed from May to September, following the manufacturer's instructions.

 This recipe will have to be emptied out every second or third year so that the hostas can be split (see page 7). Take care when emptying the box not to damage the bulbs, as these can be replanted. This is always a good opportunity to either renew the soil or to incorporate fresh peat.

18 A POT FOR THE PATIENT

This unusual combination of plants should not be attempted by those without patience. Although you can enjoy a few Winter bulbs and a hardy perennial with pretty fern-type foliage, the highspot of the recipe is unlikely to make its debut until the second year after planting.

Site
Full to partial sun and sheltered from winds.

Container
Barrel: 55cm (22″) in diameter, 40cm (16″) deep.

Plant
Late September.

Looks its best
June and eventually July.

Ingredients
  2 *Thalictrum aquilegifolium.*
  5 Madonna lilies *Lilium candidum.* Order them in August and ask for them to be dispatched as soon as they are available. Plant them as soon as you get them.
20 *Narcissus triandrus* 'Thalia'.
50 litres of John Innes No 2 or a peat-based compost.
Sufficient drainage material to cover the base of the container to a depth of 7½cm (2″).
½ bucket of horticultural grit or horticultural sand.

Method
1. Soak the thalictrum in a basin of water.
2. Put the drainage material and half the soil into the barrel.
3. Make a circle of five indentations for the lilium bulbs and just mix some of the sand or grit around in the soil upon which they are to sit. Sit them down and cover them with about 5cm (2″) of soil and then position the thalictrums in the centre of the pot. The daffodil bulbs should be grouped in clumps of four and five around the thalictrums.
4. Fill the container up with soil. Water and refill with soil if any of the soil has settled.

Aftercare
Do not let the soil become too dry although these plants are a lot less thirsty than many we have used. Feed monthly from May to September.

Tidy up the stems of the thalictrum by dead-heading after flowering and cut the whole plant down to ground level in November. Let the bulbs die down naturally after flowering. Although they do look untidy, the new growth of the thalictrum should soon overtake the daffodils' yellowing leaves.

It is difficult to establish Madonna lilies but if you succeed you will have a memorable pot to enjoy and to anticipate – for, once established, these lilies should last.

19 ELEGANT AND UNUSUAL

Putting greys and pinks together is always a sure-fire way to create a pleasant effect. This recipe is made even more elegant by using a warm cream-coloured container.

Site
Sunny and protected from cold north-easterly winds. Be prepared to give protection in severe Winters.

Container
Bowl and Pedestal. Bowl: 50cm (20″) in diameter, 20cm (8″) deep. Pedestal: 60cm (24″) high.

Plant
Late April/May.

Looks its best
Late June to October.

Ingredients
2 *Abelia* x *grandiflora*.
2 *Acaena* 'Copper Carpet'.
1 *Rosa* 'Marguerite Hilling'.
25 litres of John Innes No 3.
A broken pot or thin piece of polystyrene to cover the hole at the base of the pot.
A handful of gravel or horticultural grit as drainage material.
3 handfuls of bonemeal.

Method
1. Soak all the plants in a basin of water for at least 20 minutes.
2. Cover the hole in the bottom of the bowl with the crock or polystyrene and place the drainage material over it.
3. Put a quarter of the soil in the bowl and mix in the bonemeal.
4. Now take the rose first. If its root shape fits into the bowl, well and good. If the roots are wayward and one is particularly long, for example, shorten it with a sharp pair of secateurs. Bear the overall size of the plant in mind when you are doing this. Do not cut off too much root – certainly do not reduce the root by more than one third. Settle the roots into the soil and cover with more soil.
5. The abelia has more fibrous roots and is easier to plant. You have to lay the plant on its side to fit it into the bowl and to encourage the foliage to drape over the edge. In order not to end up with hummocks on the surface soil level, just hold the top of the root ball under a tap, or hose for a few minutes around the neck of the plant.
6. With the three main plants in position, pour about half the soil into the bowl. Fit the acaena to flow over the edge on either side of the rose.
7. Fill up and around with soil and then water thoroughly.
8. Top up any dimples in the soil level with more soil. Put a layer of horticultural grit on top – in a bowl like this it helps keep the soil underneath a little cooler by reflecting the sun; it also looks pretty.

Aftercare
Keep the soil moist and feed weekly from May to September with a specially formulated rose feed.

The abelias grow quite slowly but if the bowl becomes crowded take one of them out. Trim the abelia after it has finished flowering. Cut out dead wood or very weak stems in late March.

The acaena is a carpeter and only trails over the edge because it believes it might find some soil to root in. This of course suits our purpose very well – but it is rampant. If it is also colonizing the rest of the bowl snip some of its runners and slow down its expansion.

The rose is a modern shrub rose. This has a spread of about 17½cm (7″), so it cannot stay happily in this shallow bowl for very long unless it is cut back. After it has finished flowering in July examine the rose and cut out the dead and weak stems from the base. Then cut down any stems that have become too long (see page 8). Be prepared to move this rose to a much larger container after it has flowered twice.

Because the container is so shallow you have to pay extra attention to the soil. If it shrinks, top it up with fresh soil whatever the time of the year. In March remove the grit dressing and gently rub a handful of bonemeal into the soil. It is not really very pleasant stuff so do use rubber gloves and choose a still day. Do not let the bonemeal touch the leaves of the plant. Now put a 1cm (½″) layer of *wet* peat on top of the pot and replace the grit.

The abelia are only just hardy. In the Winter keep the pot in a sheltered position and if the weather is very severe put some polythene bubble loosely around it or wrap sacking around it.

20 BLUEBELLS AND LAVENDER

The campanula, surrounded by first year lavender spikes, makes a handsome and scented addition to this container collection.

Site
Sun or partial shade. Fairly sheltered, otherwise the campanula will blow down.

Container
Barrel or similar container: 55cm (22″) in diameter, 40cm (16″) deep.

Plant
October.

Looks its best
June/July.

Ingredients
12 small (or 5 large) lavender plants *Lavandula spica* 'Hidcote': these are less likely to get leggy.
 2 *Campanula persicifolia.*
60 litres of peat-based compost or John Innes No 2 soil.
Sufficient drainage material to cover the base of the barrel to a depth of 10cm (4″), (large lumps of polystyrene will do).
 3 handfuls of bonemeal.

Method
1. Soak all the plants in a basin of water for at least ten minutes.
2. Put the drainage material in the base of the barrel and then add half the soil. Put the handfuls of bonemeal around the edge of the barrel and mix it into the soil.
3. Loosely fill up the barrel with the rest of the soil to within 2½cm (1″) of the rim.
4. Position the campanula in the centre of the barrel.
5. Position the lavender at equal distances all around the edge.
6. Just pull back enough soil with your fingers to be able to plant each subject, keeping the neck of the plant 2½cm (1″) below the rim of the barrel.
7. Water thoroughly with at least 4 litres (1 gallon) of water and then fill in holes that appear on the surface with more soil.

Aftercare
Water regularly and feed fortnightly from June to September.

The campanula is supposed to reach a height of 90cm – which is high for an unsupported plant. If you feed it too much it will grow even taller and become floppy. Therefore do not feed till the campanula is in flower: try to circle the pot concentrating the solution on the lavender and not the campanula.

When the flower spikes of campanula die, cut them out right down to ground level to encourage more spikes. Divide the campanula when the plants become overcrowded.

When the lavender has finished flowering cut off the dead flower spikes. Trim it the following March if it has become untidy – just cut over it with sharp scissors.

21 ECHOES OF THE FLOWER BORDER

This pot is dominated by anaphalis – which is often dried and used for Winter decoration. It is not very showy but it is nice to have later-flowering plants like this one to look forward to.

Site
Sun or partial shade; it will tolerate more drought than most.

Container
Medium sized pot or tub: 40cm (16″) in diameter, 35cm (14″) deep.

Plant
October.

Looks its best
June/July/September.

Ingredients
2 *Anaphalis triplinervis.*
1 *Cotinus coggygria* 'Foliis Purpureis'.
2 *Tradescantia virginiana* 'Carmine Glow'.
25 litres of John Innes No 3 or a peat-based compost.
Sufficient drainage material to cover the base of pot to a depth of 2½cm (1″).

Method
1. Soak the plants in a saucer of water for at least ten minutes before planting.
2. Put the drainage material in the base of the container.
3. Put one third of the soil into the container.
4. Plant the cotinus first at the back of the pot.
5. Position the tradescantia and the anaphalis around the cotinus.
6. Put more soil around the plants. Water and fill up any holes on the surface, taking care to maintain the soil level 2cm (1″) below the rim of the pot.

Aftercare
Water regularly and feed fortnightly from May to September.

Trim the cotinus into shape in March. The anaphalis and the tradescantia will need to be divided after two years. This is best done in October (see page 7).

If you want to replant the cotinus into a pot you might consider pruning its roots as well as the top growth (see page 8).

22 THE WEE ONES

This beautiful strip of plants looks interesting in Winter and stunning in early Summer.

Site
Some sun.

Container
We have used a long thin box:
88cm (36″) long,
20cm (8″) deep,
20cm (8″) wide.

Plant
October.

Look its best
June.

Ingredients
2 *Saponaria ocymoides*.
1 *Armeria maritima* (thrift).
1 *Spiraea japonica* 'Little Princess'.
1 *Campanula* 'Birch Hybrid'.
1 *Viola labradorica* 'Purpurea'.
1 *Thymus* 'Doone Valley'.
1 *Veronica cinerea*.
30 litres of John Innes No 3 or a peat-based compost.
A small amount of drainage material; just a few crocks, some fine gravel or polystyrene beads.

Method
1. Soak all the plants in a basin of water.
2. Place the drainage material and half of the soil in the base of container.
3. Roughly divide the box into seven sections. If you choose to follow the order given in the line drawing remember to plant the saponaria and the campanula right up against the front of the box.
4. Fill in the gaps around the rootballs with soil and then water with at least 2 litres (½ a gallon) of water sprinkled slowly across the trough.
5. Top up the soil level where gaps appear.

Aftercare
Keep the soil most and feed monthly.
Saponaria has to be carefully restrained. After it has flowered cut off the flowered stems at ground level. This will keep it looking much tidier. In November trim it over leaving it about 5cm (2″) high. Then take a trowel and cut down through the soil all around both of the plants. This will cut off any runners that are growing.

Once the spiraea, viola and thrift begin to spread, remove the left hand saponaria altogether and re-plant it giving it more space.

The campanula's flowering stems must also be cut off after flowering, otherwise the growth becomes straggly. New stems and leaves will soon grow. If it threatens to colonize too much available space after its first year you must reduce its size.

The veronica should also be reduced in size as follows. In March take a sharp-edged trowel (or knife) and cut the plant in half right down into the soil. The half that you remove can be replanted elsewhere and should, given a little care, go on to flower. Fill any gaps you have made with soil or peat and then water thoroughly.

The spiraea, armeria, viola and thyme will fill out gradually. The armeria and thyme can be divided (see page 7) in March before the third season. When the spiraea becomes too large it is best transferred, but it will stay in a window box for at least three years. The viola grows rather more slowly. If you do feel it is becoming greedy for space divide it in March.

Renew the soil when dividing plants. If you are not emptying the box then top up with peat in March.

23 PINK, PURPLE AND PEPPERMINT

This permanent combination improves with the years.

Site
Some sun.

Container
Large wooden tub:
47½cm (19″) cubed. (A barrel will do equally well.)

Plant
October.

Looks its best
June.

Ingredients
   1 *Rosa* 'The Fairy'.
   1 *Rosa* 'Eleanor'.
   1 *Cotinus coggygria* 'Royal Purple'.
   1 *Senecio* 'Sunshine' (*S. greyi* of gardens).
  60 litres of John Innes No 3.
   2 handfuls of bonemeal.
  ¼ of an average bucket full of small pieces of polystyrene for drainage.

Method
1. Soak all the plants in a basin of water for at least ten minutes.
2. Put the drainage material in the base of the container and then add half the soil together with the bonemeal. Mix this around in the soil.
3. Place the larger of the two roses at the back left hand corner of the box – and the second rose just off centre to the right. Position the cotinus in the back left hand corner of the box. The senecio should go near the centre at the front left.
4. Put the rest of the soil around the roots and water thoroughly.
5. Fill any holes in the soil level that may appear and make sure that the corners are packed down. The plants should be about 2½cm (1″) below the rim of the box.

Aftercare
Water regularly and feed weekly. Spray for aphids weekly from June till September. Roses are unfortunately very attractive for black, green and white fly. See page 3 for advice on insecticides.

In February prune the roses lightly following the instructions given on page 8. Cut the senecio back in order to make it bush. You can be quite hard on this plant and it will still survive.

The cotinus will grow more slowly but if you need to trim it a little, cut it back in November.

This recipe will last several years. Each March take off about 2½cm (1″) of topsoil. The roots will be closely matted but try to incorporate a handful of bonemeal into the soil. Either replace the old soil with half a bucket of peat added to it, or add new soil. If you add new soil put a thin layer of wet peat on top of the new soil.

24 SIMPLE ROSES

This miniature rose makes a simple centrepiece for a medium-sized tub.

Site
Sunny.

Container
Medium sized tub:
40cm (16″) in diameter,
35cm (14″) deep.

Plant
October or March.

Looks its best
June.

Ingredients
  1 *Rosa* 'Esther's Baby'.
  1 *Gypsophila repens*.
 25 litres of John Innes No 3.
  1 handful of bonemeal.
A small amount of decorative top dressing; either horticultural grit or gravel.
A small amount of drainage material: either horticultural grit or gravel.

Method
1. Soak plants in a basin of water for at least 20 minutes.
2. Place approximately 2½cm (1″) of drainage material in the bottom of the container.
3. Now put two thirds of the soil into the container with a handful of bonemeal.
4. Put the rose in the centre of the container and position the gypsophila in front of it.
5. Pour the rest of the soil around the rose and water well. Fill up any dimples in the soil level that might appear after watering with more soil.

Aftercare
Water regularly. In a pot this size the new combined feed and insecticide pellets are the best answer for aphids and for feeding. Follow the manufacturers instructions on how many to use and how often to use them.

  This rose should not need pruning. Cut out the dead stems in March. If it throws up suckers – fast growing stems from the roots rather than the main stem – tear these right out with your hand. Do this whenever you see one.

25 SILVER YEAR ROUND

This silvery recipe is pleasing in Winter but really comes into its own in Summer. The dianthus are beautiful to look at and smell very sweetly.

Site
Sunny position.

Container
Medium sized tub: 40cm (16″) in diameter, 35cm (14″) high.

Plant
Early May.

Looks its best
June/July.

Ingredients
1 *Juniperus horizontalis* 'Blue Chip'.
2 *Dianthus* x *allwoodii* 'Doris'.
2 *Senecio cineraria* (often called *Cineraria maritima*). In colder areas it is advisable to add these plants in May to the pot.
A small amount of drainage material such as very small pieces of polystyrene.
25 litres of Arthur Bowers Ericaceous soil or Fisons Greenleaf.

Method
1. Soak all the plants in a basin of water for 20 minutes.
2. Put the drainage material in the bottom of the pot.
3. Put half the soil into the pot and mix it with the bucket of peat.
4. Plant the juniper and then the dianthus. You must be particularly careful when planting the dianthus to keep its 'neck' above soil level. If its lower leaves become wet, damp will rot the stems.
5. Make holes in the soil for the cineraria with your fingers and space them in between the other plants.

Aftercare
Water regularly and feed monthly with a general liquid feed.

The only real problem in this recipe is the dianthus which will last for only two or – at the very most – three seasons. To continue to enjoy dianthus replace the plant after its second flowering. If you lose a plant because of damp rot, pull it out and replace when you can.

The *Senecio cineraria* is almost an evergreen hardy perennial but is sold as an annual in strips. It is inexpensive so is worth risking for a Winter. If it survives a Winter the plants will get big, so pinch out its new growth. The juniperus grows very slowly and can be left alone.

Aim to replant this container with new dianthus after its second flowering. This is a good opportunity to renew the soil.

26 HOSTA WITH SCENTED LILY

By combining hostas with lilies you can have foliage, scent and flower all at once. And even in this quite small container you can underplant with Spring bulbs.

Site
Sunny with partial shade.

Container
Medium sized pot: 40cm (16″) in diameter, 35cm (14″) deep.

Plant
October.

Looks its best
July.

Ingredients
1 *Hosta* 'Royal Standard'.
1 *Hosta fortunei* 'Picta'.
3 *Lilium regale*.
40 *Muscari armeniacum*.
25 litres of a peat-based compost.
A few handfuls of polystyrene or gravel as drainage material.

Method
1. Soak the hostas in a basin full of water for at least 20 minutes.
2. Put the drainage material in the bottom of the container.
3. Put 10cm (4″) of soil into the container.
   Place the lily bulbs on the soil and cover them with a layer of soil.
4. Now position the hostas on either side of the pot. Cover with soil to within 5cm (2″) of the top of the pot and plant the muscari bulbs. The first layer of these bulbs can be pressed down into the soil and a little more soil added before the rest of the 40 bulbs are planted.
5. Now fill with soil, gently knocking the pot as you go, to within 1cm (½″) of the rim.
6. Water thoroughly and top up any dimples that appear in the soil level with more soil.

Aftercare
Water regularly. If it is difficult to keep the tub sufficiently moist, place a saucer underneath the container. Feed monthly until July; then feed fortnightly until October.

The lilies will reappear year after year and so will the muscari. To ensure good strong lily plants remove the heads of the lilies which contain seed pods after they have finished flowering. The hostas will need to be divided after every second year (see page 7).

It is a good idea to replace the soil and to sort over the muscari bulbs while dividing the hostas. This operation is best done in late September/early October. After you have pulled the hosta rootball from the pot, gently sort through the top layer of soil for the muscari bulbs. Then pull them apart making single bulbs again. Select the 40 best ones to replant.

The lilies may well have produced new bulbs too. If the lilies are becoming congested, divide the bulbs and replant the soundest and largest. The smaller ones can be planted in a pot on their own and will produce flowers when they are mature enough.

27   SHRUBBY FOLIAGE WITH ORANGE AND LEMON

Because these small shrubs tolerate trimming this permanent collection of foliage and trouble-free perennials can stay intact for two years.

Site
Some sun; sheltered from north-easterly and northerly winds.

Container
Terracotta window box: 77½cm (31″) long, 20cm (8″) wide, 18½cm (7½″) deep.

Plant
Early April.

Looks its best
Looks very nice all year but is more colourful between May and October.

Ingredients
1 *Euonymus fortunei* 'Emerald Gaiety'.
1 *Coprosma kirkii* 'Variegata'. This is sold as a houseplant and is most likely to be available from garden centres in early Spring. If you cannot get hold of it use *Hedera helix* 'Goldchild' as an alternative.
1 *Pittosporum tenuifolium* 'Abbotsbury Gold'.
2 *Geum* x *borisii*.
1 *Potentilla recta* 'Warrenii'.
25 litres of John Innes No 3.
Sufficient drainage material to cover the base of container to the depth of 1cm (½″).

Method
1. Soak all the plants in a basin for at least 20 minutes.
2. Put the drainage material in the bottom of the container and add a third of the soil.
3. Position the euonymus at the back on the left hand side. If the plant is spindly pinch out the two newest top leaves on each stem: this will make it bush. Position the pittosporum in the middle of the right hand section. The coprosma or ivy should go in a central position against the front of the box. (Our coprosma plant was in fact two separately rooted cuttings – so we split it.) The geums should go at each end of the box and the potentilla in the centre.
4. Add the remaining soil, and water thoroughly. If any gaps appear in the surface soil level, top them up. Be particularly careful to pack down the soil into the corners.

Aftercare
Water regularly and feed fortnightly from May to September using Chempak 4 or Phostrogen.

Cut out any dead wood and trim the euonymus, the pittosporum and the coprosma in late May.

After two years the geums and the potentilla will become too large for this box. Empty it and split the plants (see page 7). If you want to retain this arrangement replant it in the same way in fresh soil.

In colder areas the coprosma will need protection during freezing weather: we wrapped the trough in a piece of polythene bubble.

28 SOFT WHITE, GENTLE PINK AND A DELICATE MAUVE

This is a pretty box which you can only fully appreciate at close range: the delicately veined geraniums and the lightly scented roses make little impact from the other side of the street.

Site
Sunny window ledge.

Container
Wooden window box:
75cm (30″) long,
17½cm (7″) deep,
17½cm (7″) wide.

Plant
October.

Looks its best
June to first frost.

Ingredients
1 *Rosa* 'Petit Four'.
1 *Rosa* 'Bianca' (see the rose specialists in the back of the book).
1 *Rosa* 'Pour Toi'.
3 *Geranium cinereum* 'Apple Blossom'.
2 *Phlox subulata* 'White Delight'.
20 litres of peat-based compost.
Sufficient drainage material to cover the box to a depth of 2½cm (1″).
2 handfuls of bonemeal.

Method
1. Soak all the plants in a saucer of water for at least 20 minutes.
2. Put the drainage material in the base of the container together with a third of the soil. Spread the bonemeal over this soil and mix it in with your hand.
3. If the rose is container-grown remove it from its pot. If the roots curl all around the root ball gently tease them out to help them get established.
    Put the roses in the middle of the right hand and left hand section of the box. I have put the two smaller ones at the right hand end of the box. Place the geraniums along the front. The phlox will make a clump in between the roses.
4. Put the rest of the soil over the roots.
5. Water thoroughly and fill in any gaps in the soil level with more soil. Ensure that the soil is packed well down into the corners.

Aftercare
Water regularly and feed weekly from early May until the end of September.
    Trim the roses and cut out the dead wood – you will not have to prune these roses as such.
    Split the little geraniums by gently uprooting them and pulling them apart, then replant them. This is best done in October. There is no need to empty out the box to do this. The phlox may get a little untidy after two Summers – best really to pull them out and replant fresh ones.

29 ROSE AND LADY'S MANTLE

The rose needs a garnish around its base when it is grown in a container. *Alchemilla mollis* is easily grown and complements the very bluey crimson of this little bush.

Site
Sun or partial shade.

Container
Straight-sided pot: 40cm (16″) in diameter, 30cm (12″) high.

Plant
October or April.

Looks its best.
June.

Ingredients
1 *Rosa* 'Fairy Damsel' (see suppliers list).
3 or 4 tiny *Alchemilla mollis* (these plants seed themselves profusely and four small seedlings will do admirably) *or*
1 *Alchemilla mollis* plant (this can be divided).
20 litres of John Innes No 3 soil.
A few pieces of broken pot or thin pieces of polystyrene for drainage.

Method
1. Soak the rose for at least 20 minutes before planting.
2. Put the drainage material and one-third of the soil into the pot.
3. If the rose is container-grown just tease out a few of its roots before you position it in the centre of the pot.
4. Depending on how large the roots of the alchemilla are, either plant the alchemilla or if you have been able to get hold of little seedlings, just make holes in the surface of the filled pot for them.
5. Water thoroughly and then check for soil settlement afterwards, filling in any gaps you see.

Aftercare
This is a nice easy pot to manage. It needs little attention through the course of the year other than watering, spraying and feeding.

Keep the soil moist; feed weekly either with phostrogen or a special rose feed, and dead-head the roses as they finish flowering. Roses are liked by greenfly and other aphids so be prepared to spray with insecticide. In a pot this size you might consider using combined insecticide and fertilizer tablets – then it really is a doddle!

Each March review the alchemilla. If they were becoming too large at the end of the previous season dig the roots out of the pot with a hand fork. You will be able to see the individual plantlets. Divide them following the instructions given on page 7.

When you replant, incorporate some peat and a handful of bonemeal into the soil. As long as you do this you should be able to keep the soil in a reasonable condition for at least three years.

30 SUBSTITUTE FOR A GARDEN

This large, heavy barrel makes a home for lots of plants. Because of its shape the soil depth varies from a respectable 30cm (12″) to almost nought at the sides. While this gives the opportunity to use a tree it also means we have to plant shallow rooting succulents around the edge. We have used heathers and conifers to give Winter colour, Spring bulbs for Springtime colour and schizostylis and gentian for Autumn colour. This really is a garden in miniature providing year-round interest.

Site
Half a day's sun.

Container
Trough made out of a barrel: 85cm (34″) long, 65cm (26″) wide, 32½cm (13″) deep.

Plant
October or April.

Looks its best
September to first frost.

Ingredients
1 *Gentiana septemfida*.
1 *Chamaecyparis lawsoniana* 'Lutea Nana'.
1 *Chamaecyparis obtusa* 'Nana Gracilis'.
1 *Schizostylis coccinea* 'Major' (red).
1 *Schizostylis coccinea* 'November Cheer' (pink).
10 *Iris reticulata*.
1 *Erica cinerea* 'White Dale'.
1 *Erica carnea* 'Winter Beauty'.
1 *Calluna vulgaris* 'Blazeaway'.
1 *Sedum reflexum* (stone orpine).
1 *Sedum* 'Ruby Mantle'.
1 *Sedum oreganum* var. *procumbens*.
1 *Anagallis monelli*.

Ingredients continued

1 *Acer japonicum* 'Aureum'.
50 litres of John Innes No 3 soil.
50 litres of Levingtons Greenleaf or Arthur Bowers Ericaceous Soil.
A small amount of horticultural grit or small pieces of polystyrene for drainage.

Method

1. Soak all the plants in water while you prepare the barrel or trough.
2. Put some drainage material in the barrel bottom.

3. Now take the ericaceous soil – the soil suitable for lime-hating plants. The aim is to put a strip of this soil diagonally across the barrel with the other soil taking up the space on either side. Pieces of cardboard help to keep the soil apart while you fill it. Do try to keep the soil types separate (they will, of course, mix in time as there is no barrier to separate them). Fill the barrel to within 2½cm (1″) of the top with soil.
4. Now plant the real lime-haters in the centre of the ericaceous strip. That is the gentian, the calluna and the *Erica cinerea.* Just make holes for these plants with your fingers.
5. Plant the *Iris reticulata* – tiny little bulbs – in the John Innes soil. (Ignore this for the moment if you are planting in Spring.)
6. Plant the acer in the deepest part of the trough. Although this particular acer is not a lime-hater it will grow in the ericaceous soil.
7. Plant the other heathers where you choose.
8. Plant the sedums close to the edge of the box so that they will trail over the edge.
9. Plant the little conifers in either one of the soils.
10. Plant the schizostylis in March or April. These are best bought from a bulb specialist.
11. Put a layer of *wet* peat or wood bark on top of the soil.
12. Water thoroughly with at least one gallon of water and a watering can with a rose.

Aftercare

Keep this barrel well watered and weekly feed with phostrogen from May to September.

Each March or April remove any debris that has collected on the soil surface and if possible remove some of the top layer of soil. This will be difficult because the container is so closely planted but do what you can. Now replace this top layer with fresh peat.

All the plants will spread naturally. The sedums are easy enough to reduce in size – simply fork them from the soil and pull them apart. The conifers grow beautifully slowly and so do the acer. But the schizostylis spread quite quickly as do the heathers.

Fork up the schizostylis every second or third March and simply separate out the bulbils with their roots attached. Then replant. For the heathers it is probably best to simply remove the existing plants and to replant new ones.

The gentian will also expand quite rapidly if it is happy. It should be divided in March. (If you can really forego more of those lovely blue flowers.)

31 ONE FOR THE SCULPTURALISTS

There is a real divide amongst gardeners who like romantic scented flowers with leafy backgrounds and those that prefer the hard lines of brick and stone broken with sword-shaped plants like this one. This outline would not 'grace' anything, but a pair like this could have impact.

Site
Sunny – this plant is only just hardy even in the south-east. It needs the protection of a sheltered site and a south-facing wall in Winter.

Container
Barrel or Verseilles Tub: 39cm (15½″) cubed. This tub is just deep enough – the plant will need repotting next Spring.

Plant
April/May.

Looks its best
Looks much the same all the year.

Ingredients
 1 *Phormium tenax* 'Atropurpureum'.
 1 *Potentilla nepalensis* 'Miss Willmott'.
40 litres of a peat-based compost.
A small amount of polystyrene for drainage.

Method
1. Soak the plants in a basin of water for 20 minutes.
2. Put the drainage material and a third of the soil into the base of the container.
3. Plant the phormium and potentilla, filling in with soil around the side as you plant the potentilla. Top up with soil.
4. Water thoroughly and top up any holes that appear in the soil level with more soil.

Aftercare
The phormium needs to be kept well watered. If you want to let this planting look after itself you might consider buying one of the plastic containers available (similar in style to the one pictured) which have

water reservoirs built in. The potentilla is not averse to moisture. Feed fortnightly with a general liquid feed.

The potentilla should be cut back after it has finished flowering in August. The phormium needs little attention through the course of the year other than the removal of dead leaves.

Each March replace as much of the top soil as you can, either with new soil and a layer of peat or if you cannot remove very much soil without damaging the roots, just add a layer of peat.

Although you may buy a 1 metre (3 feet) plant they do grow quite steadily. Be prepared to repot this plant after two to three years and eventually to consign it to a garden.

32   SERENE, ROUND AND RESTFUL

This wide-mouthed saucer can accommodate lots of plants. The arrangement need never be static, with one plant giving way to others as they mature at their various paces.

Site
Sun or partial shade.

Container
Bowl: 50cm (20″) in diameter, 35cm (14″) deep.

Plant
April.

Looks its best
July/August.

Ingredients
1 *Astilbe* 'White Gloria'.
1 *Ampelopsis brevipedunculata* 'Elegans'.
1 *Lithospermum diffusum*.
1 *Pratia pedunculata* (not visible).
1 *Geranium sanguineum lancastriense* 'Splendens'.
50 litres of Fisons Greenleaf compost.
Sufficient drainage to cover the bottom to a depth of 2½cm (1″).

Method
1. Soak all the plants in a basin of water for at least 20 minutes.
2. Put the drainage material in the base of the container together with half the soil.
3. Now position the plants. The lithospermum should be placed against the edge of the pot as should the ampelopsis. The astilbe gives this arrangement height. The geranium gives pretty flowers and covers bare soil. The pratia is barely visible. Its soft blue and the lithospermum's dark blue look like sea and sky together.
4. Fill the container up with soil, and water thoroughly.

Aftercare
This is a fairly easy container to care for. Begin watering the plants with Chempak 2, Phostrogen or a general feed one month after you have planted them.

The astilles will be the first to want attention: they will need to be divided (see page 7) in March or April of the second year although they might wait until the third year.

The most interesting plant here is the ampelopsis which is related to the virginia creeper. It dies back in Winter and throws up new growth the following Spring. This effectively prevents it getting massive like its relation.

The geraniums will have to be divided in their second year but can be tackled without emptying the whole pot.

Each March tidy over the soil surface of this arrangement. Remove the top 5cm (2″) of soil and replace this with new soil.

33 STRONG GROWTH, SILVER FOLIAGE

This striking silver plant grows very vigorously. Here it is coupled with a variegated-leaf hardy plant and an attractive variegated-leaf tender plant. If you do not relish the thought of uprooting it, duplicate the hardy sage and avoid the plectranthus.

Site
At least half a day's sun is required – all silver leafed plants need a sunny spot.

Container
Terracotta trough or similar container. (A barrel would also suit very well.) Although depth is not required by the plant it would look out of proportion in a shallow container. This one is 70cm (28″) long, 32½cm (13″) deep, 30cm (12″) wide.

Plant
October or April.

Looks its best
Looks its best all the year round.

Ingredients
1 *Artemisia ludoviciana*.
1 *Salvia officinalis* 'Tricolor' (sage).
1 *Plectranthus hirtus* 'Variegatus' (Swedish ivy – in our part of the world anyway).
50 litres of peat-based compost.
Sufficient drainage to cover the base of the container to a depth of 2½cm (1″).

Method
1. Soak all the plants in a saucer of water for at least ten minutes.
2. Put the drainage material and half the soil into the container.
3. Put the artemisia in the centre of the container and the sage and plectranthus towards the front at either side.
4. Fill the container up with soil and water thoroughly.
5. Fill in any holes that appear in the soil level after it has settled.

Aftercare
These plants look after themselves very well. Feed the container monthly beginning in May but do not attempt to be generous with feed.

The most important thing to do in the Spring (whether you planted in Autumn or Spring) is to pinch out the top leaves from the artemisia. Do this as soon as it starts to show growth in April. This will encourage it to bush. Pinch out again in June.

The artemisia will have to be divided in its second year (see page 7). The sage can be left alone but after three years or so it begins to get woody stems and looks untidy. This is the time to start again with a new plant.

If you do use the plectranthus you will have to either remove it from the pot and bring it indoors in Winter. Or take cuttings from it in August and plant these in small pots in peat-based compost. Keep them in a sunny window sill and water sparingly. In May when risks of frost are over these small plants can be replaced in the container.

34   A BIG BARREL FOR TOTAL SHADE

This barrel lives against a north-east wall and gets very, very little sun. Despite that, its green framework is strong and annuals give a Summer adornment.

Site
Shaded.

Container
Large barrel: 66cm (26″) in diameter, 37½cm (15″) deep.

Plant
October.

Looks its best
February/March and July.

Ingredients
 1 *Mahonia japonica.*
 3 *Helleborus foetidus.*
 2 *Pulmonaria saccharata* 'Argentea'.
 4 *Impatiens* F1 hybrids (busy lizzie).
 2 *Pelargonium* 'Caroline Schmidt'.
15 *Narcissus cyclamineus* 'February Silver'.
48 litres of peat-based compost.
Sufficient polystyrene broken into small pieces to cover the base of the barrel to a depth of approximately 5cm (2″).
 2 handfuls of bonemeal.

Method
1. Soak all the plants in a basin of water for at least 20 minutes.
2. Put the drainage material, half the soil and a couple of handfuls of bonemeal into the barrel.
3. Plant the mahonia first. Make sure the neck of the plant will lie 2½cm (1″) below the rim of the barrel when the planting is complete. Now position the other plants around the barrel. Fill with soil around the plants to within 15cm (6″) of the rim and sit the bulbs in clumps in between the shrubs and perennials.
4. Fill the barrel up with the rest of the soil and water thoroughly so that the bulbs and the soil settles. Fill in any gaps that appear in the soil level with more soil.
5. Plant the annuals in the following May. If any

yellowing leaves from the bulbs still remain, gently pull them off so as not to damage the bulbs. Make six holes to plant the annuals.

Aftercare
This is a very easy pot to maintain. Keep it moist and feed it monthly throughout the Summer months until September: use one of the liquid feeds available. The mahonia needs a little more feed than this but if you feed the container too much the pulmonaria and helleborus will start to get indigestion! If you have the feed made up for other plants just spray a little over the leaves of the mahonia inbetween times.

Each Autumn clear the soil of any debris and pull out the annuals. If you want to keep any of the geraniums for the following year see page 127. Then remove the top 2½cm (1″) or so of soil, replacing it either with new soil or with wet peat.

In Spring deadhead the daffodils and then let the leaves die back naturally as far as you are able to before planting Summer annuals.

35 A PERMANENT CENTREPIECE WITH OPTIONAL EXTRAS

This window box has a lovely 'core' planting of euonymus and chrysanthemum. The two sides have been planted with Summer annuals this year. When the chrysanthemum is ready to be divided its offspring can take over the box.

Site
Shade with some sun.

Container
Wooden window box: 105cm (42″) long, 20cm (8″) deep, 20cm (8″) wide.

Plant
October. The chrysanthemum can be difficult to buy, so order in early October.

Looks its best
April and July/August.

Ingredients
1 *Chrysanthemum maximum* 'Snowcap'.
2 *Euonymus japonicus* 'Aureopictus'.
2 white petunias *Petunia* x *hybrida*, Grandiflora type.
1 strip dark blue *Lobelia*.
2 white upright geraniums *Pelargonium* 'Immaculata'.
30 *Narcissus cyclamineus* 'February Gold'.
35 litres of peat-based compost or John Innes No 2 soil.
Sufficient drainage material for a 1cm (½″) layer in the bottom of the container.

Method
In the Autumn:
1. Soak all the plants for at least 20 minutes.
2. Put the drainage material and half the soil in the bottom of the box.
3. Put the chrysanthemum in the centre and the two euonymus to either side.
4. Put more soil into the box until the level is between 10–12½cm (4″–5″) from the top of the box. Make indentations for the bulbs to sit in. Fill up thoroughly with soil and water.
5. Top up any gaps that appear with more soil.

In May:
1. Remove the dead foliage from the bulbs – preferably with your fingers so as not to damage the bulbs. Pull the soil aside and plant Summer annuals.

Aftercare
Keep this container moist and feed it monthly with a general liquid fertilizer. This box is not difficult to look after but it does involve an addition in May.

In the Autumn gently remove the annuals and as much of their root as you can. Firm down the soil, adding more if necessary and disturbing the bulbs as little as possible.

The chrysanthemum should need dividing in its second year. Empty the box in November and then follow the instructions on page 7. Treat the bulbs very gently. Replant the divided chrysanthemum, the euonymus and the bulbs in new soil.

36 SHADES OF BLUE AND SILVER

This window box is evergreen – which is always nice – and has two early Summer-flowering plants to kindle interest. It's an unsymmetrical mixture. Not to be recommended for those who like their arrangement balanced.

Site
Sunny window sill.

Container
Terracotta trough: 80cm (32″) long, 20cm (8″) wide, 20cm (8″) deep.

Plant
May.

Looks its best
The evergreens are always attractive but the box is at its best in July.

Ingredients
3 *Lavandula spica* 'Hidcote' (lavender).
1 *Linum perenne*.
1 *Centaurea hypoleuca simplicicaulis*.
1 *Senecio cineraria (Cineraria maritima)*.
2 *Lobelia erinus* 'Blue Cascade' (trailing lobelia).
1 *Lobelia erinus* 'Sapphire' (compact lobelia).
25 litres of peat-based compost.
A few lumps of polystyrene to put over the drainage holes.

Method
1. Soak all the plants in a basin of water for at least 20 minutes.
2. Put a few small pieces of polystyrene over the drainage holes and then add half the soil.
3. Position the lavenders first; one in the centre and one at each end of the box. Put the other perennial plants in between the lavenders. Now fill the container with soil, knocking it on the ground as you go to settle the soil. Plant the lobelia, which will be quite small, simply by making holes with your fingers, popping the plant in and firming the soil around it.
4. Water the box thoroughly and refill any gaps in the soil that appear with more soil. Make sure the soil is well settled into the corners.

Aftercare
Water regularly and feed fortnightly.

After the lavender has finished flowering cut the flower stalks off right to their base. The lobelia will not survive the Winter and unless it seeds itself – which is possible – you will have to replant the following Spring. The linum will last two or three years but no longer. The centaurea is not a rampant grower.

After a few years the lavender becomes rather woody for window boxes and troughs so although this container will require little attention during its lifetime it will need to be replanted after two or three years.

37   A POT OF BAMBOO

There is something very pleasing about bamboo in a pot. The neat clean lines of the plant are complimented by gravel and as this combination seems to require no work (which equals no mess) it is suitable for even the most tidy-minded and organised person.

Site
Some sun; sheltered from cold winds.

Container
Terracotta pot; 35cm (14″) in diameter, 30cm (12″) deep.

Plant
May.

Looks its best
August.

Ingredients
  1 *Arundinaria variegata.*
  1 *Arundinaria viridistriata.*
  1 *Raoulia australis.*
20 litres of peat-based compost.
Small amount of horticultural gravel – a little for the bottom and a little for the top.

Method
1. Soak the plants in a basin of water for 20 minutes.
2. Put the drainage material in the base of the container and about a third of the soil.
3. Position both bamboos side by side in the container. Fill in the gaps around, making sure there are no air pockets underneath the plants.
4. Plant the raoulia to one side and fill the container up with soil.

5. Water thoroughly and fill up any dimples that might appear in the soil level with more soil.

Aftercare
Keep the plants from drying out and feed monthly with a general liquid fertilizer.
  The last two Winters have been hard for bamboos but these ones have thrown up new growth each Spring. When they do start to put on growth they can increase their size rapidly. If the pot becomes overcrowded be prepared to divide the bamboos and replant them into new soil in April (see page 7).
  The raouli just creeps along the soil. If it begins to suffocate the bamboo, use a knife to separate the part you want to keep from the part you want to be rid of and then just pull out the offending part.

38   DARK SECRETS

This damp-looking box of epimedium and zantedeschia has a sombre quality. The foliage of the semi-evergreen epimedium cascades from its topmost stems and takes on beautiful tints of red and gold in Spring and Autumn.

Site
Shaded and sheltered from winds: the box should not be allowed to dry out.

Container
Home-made wooden box with new tiles cemented onto the front: 90cm (36″) long, 20cm (8″) deep, 20cm (8″) wide.

Plant
May.

Looks its best
Foliage of epimedium is good throughout most of the year. The arum lilies should flower in June/July. One of ours did and we waited as the weeks went by for the healthy looking one on the right to flower. Alas, we waited too long for its partner turned brown – and still not a peep from the chap on the right.

Ingredients
3 *Epimedium* x *rubrum*.
1 *Zantedeschia aethiopica* 'Crowborough'.
30 litres of peat-based compost or John Innes No 2.
Smallish pieces of polystyrene to put over and around the drainage holes (if you are making the box then five drainage holes will be quite enough).

Method
1. Order and start into growth the zantedeschia as in Method 1 in the recipe 'Bleeding Hearts and White Lilies' on page 18.
2. In May soak both the plants in a basin of water for 20 minutes.
3. Put the drainage material around and over the holes in the bottom of the container. Put about 5cm (2″) of soil into the box.
4. Position the epimediums evenly across the box and the zantedeschia in between them.
5. Fill around the plants with soil and then water thoroughly.
6. Fill in any dimples that appear in the soil level with more soil. Be particularly careful that the corners of the box are well filled.

Aftercare
The most important thing to do with this box is keep it well watered – do not let it dry out during the Summer. Continue watering the box during the Winter, concentrating on the epimediums. Let the lilies be a little drier. Feed it weekly from May to August with general purpose liquid fertilizer.

The lilies will certainly need protection in the Winter. Put some grit around their stems in the window box itself and when the weather is severe put polythene bubble around the whole box, wrapping it up on top (like you would wrap pastry over a cornish pasty) and stapling it together.

Each March remove a few centimetres (or inch or two) of top soil and replace this with peat. When the epimediums begin to grow too large for this box they can be divided (see page 7). This should be done between September and March.

39   A SUNNY SUMMERY RECIPE

These coreopsis are really the froth in this good basic evergreen display. They make a very welcome bright golden yellow splash. One or two hyacinths in similar golds and oranges set off the Winter foliage.

Site
Sunny.

Container
Barrel: 56cm (22″) in diameter, 40cm (16″) high.

Plant
October.

Looks its best
May and July/August.

Ingredients
2   *Coreopsis* 'Mayfield Giant'.
2   *Lonicera pileata.*
1   *Vinca minor* 'Argenteovariegata'.
75   litres of peat-based compost.
2   Hyacinths 'Gypsy Queen' and 'City of Harlem'.
Sufficient drainage material to cover the bottom to the depth of 2½cm (1″).

Method
1. Soak all the plants in a basin of water for at least 20 minutes.
2. Put the drainage material and half the soil into the barrel, followed by the lonicera, the vinca and more soil. Position the coreopsis at the centre rear and space the hyacinths out over the barrel. The hyacinths should be planted 10cm (4″) from the soil surface so that they have 5cm (2″) of soil above their heads.
3. Fill up with the remaining soil and water thoroughly. When the soil has settled, fill up any surface gaps with more soil.

Aftercare
Although it is not advisable to neglect any plant in a container, this arrangement needs less attention than most. Water it three or four times a week if it has not rained and feed it fortnightly.

The lonicera can be trimmed like a hedge: cut it back in April when it gets too big. Also cut out the dead wood and any crossing stems. Try to let the bulbs die back of their own accord. They are untidy but they have a much better chance of a second performance next Spring if you leave them alone. Give the container its first feed of the season after the hyacinths have died.

The coreopsis and the vinca will need to be divided after two or three years – although this is a major task it must be done (see page 7). Allow yourself as much space as you can and empty the barrel. This is a good opportunity to replace the soil and to cut back the roots of the lonicera.

40 PINK FONDANT AND FEATHERY FOLIAGE

The feathery foliage of the fennel is as dainty a partner as you could find for these very delicate and sweetly scented roses.

Site
Sunny and sheltered.

Container
Terracotta vase. 55cm (22″) in diameter, 42½cm (17″) deep.

Plant
May.

Looks its best
July to August.

Ingredients
  2 *Rosa* 'Grouse' (see list of specialists).
  1 packet of Bronze Fennel seeds.
75 litres of peat-based compost.
Sufficient drainage to cover the bottom of the pot to a depth of 2½cm (1″).

Method
1. Soak the roses in water for 20 minutes.
2. Put the drainage material and several centimetres (a few inches) of soil into the container.
3. Now fit the roses into the container. If the roses are pot-grown just top the vase up with soil. If the roses are bare-rooted, scoop the soil over the roots, knocking the vase against the ground underneath as you go to settle the soil over the roses' roots.
4. Fill the pot up with soil and then water thoroughly. Fill up any dimples that are left in the soil level.
5. If it is possible, stand the pot in a basin of water for half an hour.
6. Now put the five or six fennel seeds on top of the wet compost.
7. Cover the seeds with a thin layer of compost following the instructions on the seed packet and then water very gently with a small handspray or a watering can with a fine rose.

Aftercare
Keep the pot moist and water regularly. The fennel particularly can use up a lot of water on a hot day. Begin feeding the plants a month after you have planted them with a general liquid feed.

The fennel are annuals and are best removed at the first frost. Replant them in the same way the following year as you did in the first. It's really much easier just to pop a few seeds in the centre of an arrangement than grown plants, so do not be discouraged.

The roses may well suffer from blackfly and greenfly. You can try just picking the insects from the buds which is a much superior way of getting rid of them than spraying chemicals around. If you have difficulty controlling the fly and need to use an insecticide, choose an aerosol which allows you to use only as much as you need and keep the rest.

41   AN ACQUIRED TASTE

This grey leafed fuchsia is difficult to mix with other plants. Its foliage deadens green and looks drained beside purple tones. But however awkward, it is undeniably eye catching. The right kind of backdrop – perhaps crumbling stone walls and mossy steps – could help to enhance its qualities.

Site
Sunny. In severe winters this pot should be given protection so that the roots do not get frozen.

Container
Small terracotta pot: 30cm (12″) in diameter, 25cm (10″) deep.

Plant
April.

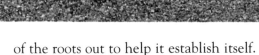

Looks its best
The foliage is attractive all year. Flowers are borne in July/August.

Ingredients
   1 *Fuchsia magellanica* 'Versicolor'.
   1 *Acaena* 'Copper Carpet'.
  15 litres of a peat-based compost.
   2 handfuls of gravel for drainage.

Method
1. Soak both the plants in a basin of water.
2. Put the drainage material and half the soil into the container.
3. If the fuchsia is a little rootbound, just tease a few of the roots out to help it establish itself.
4. Fill the soil around the fuchsia and plant the acaena against one edge of the pot.
5. Add the rest of the soil. Water thoroughly and fill in any dimples that might have appeared in the soil level.

Aftercare
This is a very easy pot to care for.
Water regularly and feed monthly beginning one month after you have planted and continuing until early September.
   The fuchsia will not grow very large. The acaena will feel frustrated in this small pot but it can do little damage.

42   A BIG SPRAWLING BARREL

This barrel has had various plants added to it – but over time only the little garnishes around the base have really stayed the course. The others have been beaten by the lavatera. It is hardy so you can cut it back and it will reliably throw up a display like this. So it's not to be scorned.

Site
Partial shade but some sun necessary.

Container
Barrel: 60cm (24″) in diameter, 40cm (16″) deep.

Plant
October.

Looks its best
July.

Ingredients
1 *Lavatera olbia* 'Rosea'.
Several *Campanula* 'Birch Hybrid' or *Campanula portenschlagiana* (this is the most invasive of the campanulas).
15 hyacinths – whatever colour suits.
80 litres of peat-based soil.
Sufficient drainage material to cover the base to a depth of 2½–5cm (1–2″).

Method
1. Soak the plants in water for 20 minutes.
2. Put the drainage material and two-thirds of the soil into the barrel.
3. Plant the lavatera first and then when the soil level is 15cm (6″) from the top of the barrel stop and position the hyacinth bulbs. These look more attractive spaced out fairly evenly across the barrel.
4. Cover with soil and then position the campanula. These should go right up against the side of the barrel.
5. Now fill the barrel up to within 2½cm (1″) of the rim and water thoroughly. Fill in any dimples in the soil level that appear after you have watered.

Aftercare
Keep the pot moist but do not worry too much about feeding this one. Feed after the hyacinths have flowered with a general liquid feed and then again when the lavatera are at the peak of their flowering.

Let the hyacinths die back naturally as far as you can – the growing foliage of the lavatera will eventually hide them.

Cut off the flowered stems of the campanula back to base level after they have finished flowering. The lavatera can be cut back each March to within several centimetres (a few inches) of the soil level. If you do not cut is back it will get straggly and woody.

This recipe will go on and on. When you are cutting back the lavatera is a good time to clear the debris from the top of the container and renew the top centimetres or inch or two of soil. Use more peat-based compost or ordinary peat.

43   A FROTHY HYDRANGEA

This smashing hydrangea comes from a cutting and so we cannot give you the precise name. Hydrangeas are very good container garden plants. They are almost evergreen and very showy in flower.

Site
Several hours of sun are required. Best if this is not early morning sun.

Container
Large barrel: 60cm (24″) in diameter, 40cm (16″) deep.

Plant
October.

Looks its best
July to August.

Ingredients
1 pale pink *Hydrangea macrophylla*, such as 'Madame E Mouilliere'.
2 *Bergenia cordifolia*.
2 *Vinca major* 'Elegantissima'.
1 *Jasminum officinale*.
90 litres of John Innes No 3 or a peat-based compost.
Sufficient drainage to cover the base of the barrel to a depth of 2½cm (1″).
Hydrangea colourant – if you want a strong pink or blue.

Method
1. Soak all the plants for 20 minutes in a basin of water.
2. Put the drainage material together with half the soil into the bottom of the barrel. If you want a strong pink, or a strong blue flower then put the hydrangea colourant into the soil at this stage.
3. Plant the hydrangea first and then put some more soil into the barrel. The bergenia and vinca are likely to come in quite small pots so do not drown them in soil.
4. Fill the barrel up to within 2½cm (1″) of the top and water thoroughly. After the soil has settled fill any dimples left in the soil surface with more soil.
5. Ensure this barrel is kept moist for the following fortnight until the hydrangea has become established: hydrangeas do like moist soil.

Aftercare
Water regularly and feed fortnightly with Phostrogen or Chempak 3. Clear the debris from the soil surface each March and replace the top 2½–5cm (1–2″) of soil with peat.

There is quite a lot of room for the plants to expand although the bergenia will need to be divided at some point. Vincas have a lovely habit of staying manageable but if they do get too large divide them between September and March (see page 7).

The hydrangea will grow, but like the vincas it seems to accept the limitations of its pot. It should be thinned out in March and have its weak shoots removed. If the plant has become too large, reduce its overall size as well.

At the very back of this photograph you can just see the thick rope-like stem of the jasmine. This was cut back by a site carpenter to let a painter reach a window. It is still alive though.

HANGING BASKETS

Why put perennials in hanging baskets? Some of the plants will survive from year to year (though in theory they all should) and it is a challenge to find something different that will grow in hanging baskets. All of these baskets have a framework of perennial plants. One or two have had Summer additions made to them. In Winter keep your hanging baskets either out in their permanent resting place which has got to be a sheltered south-facing wall if they are to survive the Winter or else drop them into a large container filled with peat and put this container against a south-facing or south-west facing wall. In most of the permanent hanging baskets we have planted a dwarf yellow daffodil, *Narcissum cyclamineus*, 'Tête-à-tête'. This is an excellent small, long lasting daffodil and it will grow in hanging baskets. In the annual baskets there are masses of bulbs. In the permanent ones – because space is limited – we have only used five or six. This is enough to be exciting to watch, especially as the foliage of the other plants unfurls.

PREPARING THE HANGING BASKET

We always use wire or plastic coated wire baskets because they look nicer than the plastic bowl types. We generally use 35cm (14″) baskets. This is a good size because it gives adequate room for quite a few plants without being unwieldy. We line the basket with moss – again because it looks nice. The moulded peat liners available are very effective and used inside a wire basket are preferable to plastic baskets. Buy moss either as wreathing moss from a florist or from garden centres where it is sold in small packets, or you can use thick lawn moss. (If there is enough to line a hanging basket it means the lawn is in terrible shape!) Buy enough moss to fill the basket up loosely. Now line the basket thickly. Make a collar right round the rim to help keep the soil in the basket when you water it. Cut a circle of polythene

with the same diameter as the hanging basket and put this on top of the moss.

PLANTING THE BASKET

If you want to grow plants out of the side of the basket now is the time to make slits in the polythene and gently push the foliage of the plant through the polythene and then through the wire. If you do not intend to plant through the sides of the basket make one drainage hole in the polythene. The reason for this polythene lining is that the moss will not last indefinitely. When the time comes to replace it, it is much easier to lift out the plants if there is a polythene layer around them.

Half fill the basket with compost. You will need between five and ten litres. If you are going to move the basket around you should use a peat-based compost.

Next position the plants. The trailers should of course be in a position to trail. The central plant should be about 30cm (12″) high, otherwise the basket looks rather flat. Once you have positioned all the plants fill the basket up with the rest of the soil and water thoroughly and slowly. Because hanging baskets dry out so quickly it is a good idea to water twice a day for a week or so after planting – even if the weather is cool – so that the plants can get established.

AFTERCARE

The simplest way to feed the hanging basket is to use combined feed and insecticide pellets. This has the added bonus of destroying aphids as well and they are not harmful to bees. These pellets cannot, however, be used on food crops, so do not put them on the herb basket.

Filling plastic and fibre moulded hanging baskets avoids using moss. Make sure the container has a hole in it and then fill with compost and plants.

44 VARIEGATED LEAF SNOBS ONLY

Over the last few years lots of people have become interested in plants with variegated leaves. Here is a very simple basket with little else but leaf.

Site
Sunny – against a south or south-west facing wall.

Container
Hanging basket: 35cm (14″) in diameter.

Plant
October.

Looks its best
Summer months.

Ingredients
1 *Ajuga reptans* 'Rainbow'.
1 *Ajuga reptans* 'Burgundy Glow'.
Saxifraga x *umbrosa* 'Variegata' (London Pride).
1 *Ophiopogon planiscapus* 'Nigrescens'.
A few mesembryanthemums for Summer colour.
15 litres of peat-based compost.

Method
1. Soak the plants in a basin of water for five minutes.
2. Prepare the hanging basket as described on page 56.
3. Put the ajuga plants in the basket and carefully pull the leaves through the holes in the polythene so that they protrude from the sides and bottom of the basket.
4. Fill the basket up to the top with soil.
5. Plant the other plants in the top, making sure the container looks well-balanced.
6. Add more moss if necessary to make a thick collar at the top of the basket. This is important as it helps to retain the soil.
7. Water well and add more soil if necessary.

Aftercare
The ajuga adapts well to growing between the wire and out of the side. Water regularly and place the pellets in the basket for feed. This arrangement is unlikely to be much troubled by insects as none of them seem over keen on the main ingredients.

The ajuga spreads rapidly from runners. To keep the whole basket evenly covered break off the plantlets at the end of the runner and pop them into the soil where they will root.

In March rebuild the sides of the basket with extra moss and put new compost on top.

45 SEDATE DARK CRIMSON

This hanging basket is much more like a traditional one – except that it is planted completely with shrubs and hardy perenniels.

Site
Sun or partial shade although like the others it will require the shelter of a south or south-west facing wall in the Winter.

Container
Hanging basket: 35cm (14″) in diameter.

Plant
October.

Looks its best
July.

Ingredients
Veronica spicata 'Red Fox'.
Dianthus deltoides (maiden pinks).
  1 *Hypericum* x *moserianum* 'Tricolor'.
  1 *Sedum sieboldii* 'Mediovariegatum'.
  1 *Hedera helix* 'Goldchild'.
  5 *Narcissus cyclamineus* 'Tête-à-tête'.
15 litres of peat-based compost.

Method
1. Soak the plants in a basin of water for five minutes.
2. Prepare the hanging basket as described on page 56.
3. Put the dianthus in the basket and carefully pull the leaves through the holes in the polythene.
4. Fill the basket up with soil.
5. Plant the rest of the plants and the bulbs in the top.
6. Add more moss if necessary to make a thick collar at the top of the basket to help to retain the soil.
7. Water well, adding more soil if necessary.

Aftercare
Water this basket daily in hot weather. Use combined feed and insecticide pellets for choice simply because they are so easy to use.

    The young shoots of the veronica seem to attract greenfly but otherwise the recipe is fairly trouble-free. This basket is best separated out in November when the veronica and the ivy can be divided. The hypericum is not fully hardy so do be prepared to give this basket Winter protection in the form of polythene bubble.

46   HERBS STRUNG UP

It is quite a good idea to grow herbs in a hanging basket whether it is because you have no alternatives or because your soil is too heavy for the Mediterranean-type aromatic plants. The marjorams, oreganos and basils which like a well drained and very light soil seem to do well in baskets.

Site
Sunny south or south-west facing wall.

Container
Hanging basket: 40cm (16″) in diameter.

Plant
Early May/May when the risk of frost is over.

Looks its best
July.

Ingredients
Basil grown from seed *Ocimum basilicum.*
   1 *Helichrysum angustifolium* (curry plant).
   1 *Origanum vulgare* (common marjoram).
   1 *Origanum vulgare* 'Aureum' (golden marjoram).
   1 *Mentha* x *gentilis* 'Variegata' (ginger mint).
   1 *Mentha rotundifolia* (apple mint).
   1 *Mentha piperita* 'Crispa' (black peppermint).
   1 *Chrysanthemum parthenium* 'Aureum' (feverfew).
 20 litres of peat-based compost.

Method
1. Prepare the hanging basket as above.
2. The marjorams and the ginger mint will grow from the side of the basket.
3. Either buy a basil plant in May when they are widely available or plant a few basil seeds where you want the basil to grow in the basket. As long as no frosts cut them back you will have edible basil by mid-July. Follow the instructions on the packet on how to sow the seeds.

Aftercare
Water daily and feed with Phostrogen, Chempak 3 or Liquinure. Pinch out the growing shoots of all the mints to encourage to them to bush. If you find the curry plant getting a little tall just trim it by up to a third. New growth from side shoots will soon cover the scars. The marjoram is a perennial and will survive the Winter but all the other plants are best treated as annuals.

47   A ROSE HANGING BASKET

This is a delightful hanging basket. Wouldn't it grace a wedding?

Site
Against a sunny wall.

Container
Hanging basket: 35cm (14″) in diameter with a sturdy 27½cm (11″) wall bracket.

Plant
March.

Looks its best
Mid-June/July.

Ingredients
  2 *Rosa* 'Fairyland'.
  3 *Viola* x *wittrockiana* (pale lilac pansies).
1/2 strip *Lobelia erinus* 'String of Pearls'.
15 litres of peat-based compost.

Method
1. Soak the roses in a basin of water for 20 minutes.
2. Prepare the hanging basket as described above.
3. Take the roses and shake any loose soil from the rootball. Put them side by side in the basket making sure that the join between the rootstock and the bush is below the level of the rim of the hanging basket. If there is one very long root – do not be afraid to cut it back. Do not reduce it by more than two-thirds of its length.
4. Carefully add compost between the roots bringing the level up to within 1½cm (½″) of the rim of the basket.
5. Plant the violas towards the back of the basket and the lobelia at the front so that it can cascade over the side.
6. Make sure the container looks well balanced and that all the plants are firmly in place.
7. Add more moss if necessary to make a thick collar at the top of the basket. This is important as it helps to retain the soil.
8. Water well and add more soil if necessary.

Aftercare
Water generously. In hot weather water daily and even twice daily. Half a watering can is about right for a mature basket. Water it with patience letting the first taste soak in and then adding more. If you water all at once it will run straight through the basket taking soil with it.

Deadhead the roses by removing the faded blooms and their stems back to a leaf joint or axil – do not leave stem spikes sticking out.

This is a suitable basket for a combined insecticide and feed pellet. After the roses have finished flowering and the basket is past its best – this will be August/September – either dismantle the basket and pot the roses onto a bigger container, or remove the lobelia and violas, stand the basket in a saucer (this is simply to make watering less onerous) and put it in an out of the way spot till the weather becomes severe. Then remove it from the saucer and put it into a larger bowl or barrel filled with peat, grit or compost. Start feeding the roses again the following May and with care you will have an even better display the next year.

STRAWBERRY POTS

Strawberry or parsley pots are a useful alternative to ordinary tubs. They are a little taller and look particularly attractive amongst groups of containers. You can also limit the growth of the more invasive plants like campanula. When buying these pots try to find some with nice deep semi circular cups around the curve of each hole. If they just have a slightly curving lip the soil tends to pour out of the pots when you water them. The planting is done in the same way in each pot – so here is a description of the *method* of planting followed by the *recipes*.

Method
1. Find a 60cm (24″) length of circular cardboard – the inside of a roll of material is ideal – or else curl a piece of cardboard into a cylinder and stick it round with sellotape.
2. Put a crock or piece of thin polystyrene across the hole in the bottom of the pot together with about 2½cm (1″) of drainage material.
3. Place the cylinder in the middle of your strawberry pot (it helps to have somebody hold it for you) and now start to put the appropriate soil around the edge of the cardboard until you come up to the level of the first hole.
4. Put your less precious plants or the easiest to grow in the bottom holes because these always seem to do less well.
5. Wash the roots of the plants to remove excess soil and then slip the roots through the hole into the pot. Spread them out and cover them with soil.

6. Work around the pot from bottom to top, planting and filling with soil until you get to within 5–7½cm (2–3″) of the top of the pot. Now pour some good fine drainage material into the centre of the pot – either horticultural grit, or horticultural quality sand.
7. Pull out the cardboard cylinder very carefully and then fill the pot to within half an inch of the rim with the appropriate soil.
8. Plant the top.
9. Water very gently to start with. Use just a small quantity of water – up to a litre (or a pint or two) – and water again that day.
10. Soil will almost inevitably spill out of the pot until the plants get established so take real care in the first week after planting to keep your pot in the warmest, most congenial place for making growth, and water it daily.
11. If the weather is dry and you are finding it difficult to keep the pot moist then place it in a saucer.

A Note on Decorative Strawberry Pots
These pots are eyecatching and fun to make up. If you want to fill all the holes first time around then do, but remember that you will have to turn the pot around weekly if all the plants are to establish. The Sedums grow very quickly and so even if you do not fill all the holes initially you will be able to fill them very soon by breaking off pieces of Sedum and just pushing them into the holes. Then you have to turn the container around.

48 READY FOR THE STEWPOT

This container gives fresh parsley, thyme, sage and mint right outside the kitchen all summer. Although parsley is a biennial it is best eaten in the first year and grown as an annual.

Site
Sun or partial shade but at least possibility of six or seven hours sun required.

Plant
Early May.

Looks its best
June/September.

Container
Parsley pot: 42½cm (17″) high, and 27½cm (11″) in diameter at its widest point.

Ingredients
1 *Petroselinum crispum* (parsley) plant.
1 packet of parsley seeds 'Extra Fine Moss Curled'.
1 French Parsley plant.
1 *Ocimum basilicum* 'Purpureum' (dark opal basil).
Thymus 'Doone Valley'.
Thymus vulgaris (common thyme).
Thymus x *citriodorus* 'Silver Queen'.
Origanum vulgare (common marjoram).
30 litres of John Innes No 2.
5–10 litres of drainage material.

Method
1. Prepare the parsley pot as in the general instruction. Position the plants around the uppermost holes, reserving the common thyme and the purple basil for the top.
2. Plant two parsley seeds in the remaining holes around the bottom of the pot.
3. Water carefully as described above.

Aftercare
Water regularly and feed weekly with Phostrogen. Make frequent use of the parsley taking care to cut the stems with sharp scissors right at the base. In the Autumn move the pot to the most congenial and sheltered position you can give it.

The thyme and marjoram will survive as will the more ornate varieties of thyme but the parsley will have to be re-sown and replanted every year. And the basil will have to be re-planted or re-grown from seed as well.

49 BRIMMING FULL

This strawberry pot is overflowing with campanula but there are plenty of other plants to sustain your interest when the campanula is cut back. Although the succulents look as if they would be more at home in a desert, this selection is not only hardy but evergreen.

Site
Sunny.

Plant
October.

Container
Strawberry pot.

Looks its best
May.

Ingredients
 1 *Dianthus* 'Little Jock'.
 1 *Crassula sarcocaulis*.
 1 *Sedum sieboldii* 'Mediovariegatum'.
 1 *Thymus* 'Doone Valley'.
 1 *Sedum spathulifolium* 'Cape Blanco'.
 1 *Sedum oreganum* var. *procumbens*.
 1 *Campanula* 'Birch Grove'.
30 litres of soil or John Innes No 2 soil.
 5 litres of horticultural sand or horticultural grit.
A crock or flat piece of polystyrene to place over the bottom of the drainage hole.

Method
Follow the instructions for filling the pot and planting given in the introduction. Put the crassula, sedum and the dianthus in the top.

Aftercare
Water regularly and feed fortnightly. All these plants will survive from year to year.

The campanula can be trimmed back after flowering just to tidy it up – it will soon make new growth. If it does become crowded in its growing area then, to avoid having to empty the pot, just take a sharp knife and cut out half the plant. This is best done in November when there is a good chance that the piece you remove will take root. Water after replanting.

The sedums are very easy to propagate – just break pieces off and with a small twig peg them into another hole.

50 A SECOND DECORATIVE POT

This second decorative pot features more examples of plants that suit this kind of pot. They are a little rarer than the plants found in the first pot – but they are to be found in small nurseries around the country and from specialists in alpine plants.

Site
Sunny.

Container
Strawberry pot.

Plant
October or April.

Looks its best
May/June.

Ingredients
    2 *Papaver alpinum.*
    1 *Alyssum saxatile.*
    1 *Alchemilla conjuncta.*
    1 *Tanacetum densum.*
    2 *Dianthus* x *calalpinus* 'Whatfield Joy'.
    1 *Hypericum olympicum.*
    1 *Sedum kamschaticum* 'Variegatum'.
    1 *Campanula cochlearifolia* 'Hallii'.
30 litres of peat-based compost.
Fine horticultural gravel.

Method
Plant the strawberry pot in the same way as described above and following the same rules. Put the alchemilla, the tanacetum and the hypericum in the top holes where the pot is widest giving them the best chance of survival. The alyssum is very easy to grow and divide and can be used to fill up the lower holes. I have put the dianthus in the top because they make such a lovely hummock with the campanula which will trail over the edge.

Aftercare
Water regularly and feed monthly. These lovely little plants are all quite tough and you need do little to them. As the flowers on each campanula stem are over nip out the stem right at the base. This will encourage it to produce more flowers. I leave the dead poppy heads on because they look pretty. The arrangement should last at least two years.

AUTUMN, WINTER AND SPRING RECIPES

INTRODUCTION TO THE
AUTUMN, WINTER AND SPRING RECIPES

The period from October to the end of April is a long time, especially during those dreary weeks of mid-Winter. Nothing we can suggest will give you brilliant displays in the depth of Winter. However, we can give you lots of ideas for colour in the Autumn and Spring so that this often forgotten period can become a time to relish your garden containers.

AUTUMN COLOUR

We have suggested the use of cyclamen, solanum, hebes, primulas and pansies for Autumn colour. These may be bought from your local garden centre and often from greengrocers. Solanum, hebes, pansies and primulas are prone to suffer from drought, so be sure to buy healthy plants. Cyclamen should have sturdy foliage and lots of buds emerging underneath so that they should continue flowering for months. In certain parts of the country the weather will be too severe to use any of these plants but in milder sheltered areas they are all worth a try. If you are dubious, choose a site closest to the house. A south or west-facing window-sill is usually your best bet. You should expect the cyclamen to die by the end of the year. (Having said that, we were lucky a few winters ago and enjoyed them right through until May, even on a north-facing windowsill. That was a rare bonus.) In severe weather, such as the early

months of 1986, some of the hebes and even some of the ivies died. Just act with faith, and if necessary replace with other plants in the Spring. The plants that do survive may be planted out elsewhere for the Summer months and used again in the following Autumn. By then they will all be bigger and may need trimming back or dividing. But for one more season at least you may like to enjoy the larger plants.

SPRING COLOUR

Wallflowers, arabis, aubrieta, forget-me-nots and alyssum are all used for Spring colour. They can be purchased from a good garden centre in September or October. You will be surprised by how much growth these will all make by the time they flower. Take care of wallflowers: if you buy them in a bundle with their roots bare, give them a good drink and plant them as soon as possible. They may look bedraggled but they should soon perk up. Alternatively, you may be able to buy them growing in strips.

But it is bulbs which are the obvious choice for Spring. Our selection mainly includes dwarf varieties which are particularly suitable for containers. We have used those varieties which we have found to be sturdy, reliable and long-lasting, and we make frequent use of the multiheaded kinds which provide such good value in an area where there is limited planting space.

We recommend that bulbs are bought as soon as they become available in the garden centres and shops, usually in early September. Although you may not need to plant them for another month they will come to no harm if they are kept in a cool, dry place. It is best to buy early so as to be sure to get the varieties you particularly want to use. All the bulbs named in the following recipes may be obtained from garden centres which sell bulbs supplied by O.A. Taylor and Sons Bulbs Ltd. Otherwise use the Mail Order specialists listed in the back of this book, but order early – by mid-September at the latest.

You may be surprised by the number of bulbs we have used in the recipes. In all instances we have tried to create a full display and the results are there to be witnessed, but you can try using less if you like. When it comes to the end of Spring you may wonder what to do with all the bulbs. We do not recommend that they are used again in containers in the following Autumn. You could simply throw them away or plant them in the garden. See the following section on Guidance for End of Season Care.

CONTINUITY OF INTEREST

Quite a few of the recipes have Autumn flowering plants such as cyclamen, solanum and primulas underplanted with bulbs. This means that you can enjoy both Autumn colour and a Spring display in the same container. In a few cases we even provide two photographs so that you can see them in both seasons. Continuity of interest is an important theme in many of these recipes. In some cases it extends from Autumn to Spring; in others it stretches from early to late Spring with the use of early and late bulbs side by side, or rockplants and primroses, etc which continue to flower over a long period.

INSTANT DISPLAYS

Unless you buy growing bulbs in early Spring you will only be able to obtain a bulb display by planting in the previous Autumn. For those who do not think ahead, we have given some ideas on instant displays. They include calceolarias and cinerarias which people often think can only be used as indoor plants. Well, in the milder sheltered districts, they can be used in all kinds of containers, from hanging baskets to Versailles tubs. We also include cowslips, bellis daisies and polyanthus which can look charming. Instant planting can be extremely colourful and very good value.

CLIMATE

Climate obviously plays a vital role in gardening. Winter frosts and biting winds could damage both bulbs and the plants. You can minimise these effects by placing your containers in sheltered parts for the worst of the Winter. Close to the house or on a window sill away from the north and east winds will do much to protect them. Then you bring them into their flowering positions in the early Spring when the weather is kinder and the new growth is evident.

WATERING

Odd as it may seem, you may need to water your Winter containers quite regularly. Window boxes often remain quite dry even though it has rained incessantly. The reason is that they may be in a rain shadow from the house. Bulbs need moisture when they are producing roots as well as when they start to send up their shoots. Lack of it will cause severe stunting. So keep a watch on the soil moisture and do not let it get too dry. Take care however never to water in frosty weather or indeed if frost threatens. Plants will not relish sitting in ice.

CONTAINERS

Our choice of containers is deliberately restricted. We have not gone out of our way to use especially glamorous containers or settings, and have concentrated on the usual window boxes, pots, barrels and urns. Dwarf bulbs and low plants can of course go in any of these containers but beware of putting the taller varieties into the smaller containers. Tall daffodils and tulips would look strange in a small window box. Adherence to scale is most important.

We did, however, test a few hanging baskets which are often not recommended for this time of year. Ours not only managed to survive a terrible Winter but provided beautiful displays in the Spring. One of the best things about them is that they are raised from the ground and displayed at eye level, often close to the front door where they can be fully enjoyed. We used a few wicker baskets as well. Given a thorough coating of yacht varnish these were unhurt by the Winter weather and produced marvellous blooms in the Spring. The basketry looked very attractive with the flowers, and could be easily moved. They make ideal presents.

Continuity of interest, instant planting schemes and interior design ideas are all evident in the chapter which follows. Try the recipes out for yourselves, adapt them to your own containers, change the colour schemes if you like. Above all experiment.

GUIDANCE FOR END OF SEASON CARE

ARABIS, AUBRIETA, ALYSSUM These should all be moved to a well drained sunny position in the garden, cut back severely and left until the Autumn when they can be used again.

BULBS It is possible to dry them off at the end of their growing period and store them through the Summer, but, in the following Autumn, only use the biggest ones and do not expect as good a display as the previous year. On the whole we do not recommend their use a second time round in containers. Our advice is to enjoy them in the garden instead, in which case continue to water the containers after flowering until such time as the bulbs can be conveniently moved. (If you do not possess a garden of your own, try to find a friend who would welcome them). The most convenient time to uproot bulbs is the middle to end of May when you will be wanting to replant the containers for the Summer. Dig a hole as deep as the container and carefully transfer the entire contents. The bulbs will all stand a better chance of survival if their roots are left as intact as possible · and their leaves and stems remain unbroken. Take particular care with tulips which will suffer badly from broken limbs.

HEATHERS The *Erica arborea* (tree heath) used in the pedestal displays have such a wonderful colour foliage that they are a worthy subject for a Summer as well as a Winter display. Prune lightly after flowering.

HEBES These should survive most Winters. Like the solanums they should be potted up or removed to the garden after the main display is over. In Spring cut them back to within 8cm (3") of the base to encourage a good bushy shape.

IVIES These often look good in Summer displays as well as the Winter ones and so may be left in the container, particularly if it is a chimney pot. Equally they may be transferred to the garden for their Summer holidays. They will tolerate most positions. You may like to tidy them up if they have become straggly over the Winter. Don't be afraid to cut them back, they will soon make new growth.

PRIMULAS, POLYANTHUS, PRIMROSES AND COWSLIPS Remove them to the garden where they can grow and be kept for another display the following season. Cowslips enjoy a sunny position; the others will thrive in shade so long as they have plenty of moisture. In time you may wish to divide them but for one more season you might like to enjoy the larger plants.

SOLANUMS These may survive the Winter although their berries will have long since shrivelled. If you want the plant for another season, pot it up or, better still, transfer it to the garden so that it can flower and produce berries again in due course. If it survives a couple of seasons you will find it has grown too large for its original containers. The time to prune is in Spring before the new growth starts. You can be quite ruthless and cut it back to within 8cm (3") of the base.

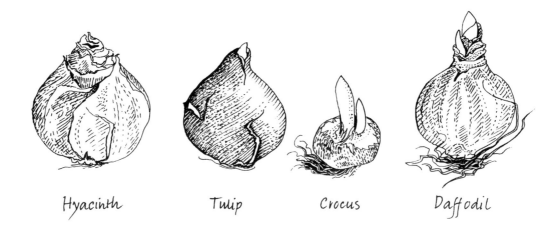

Hyacinth   Tulip   Crocus   Daffodil

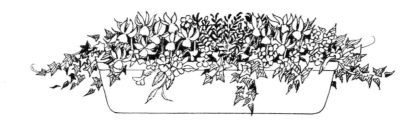

AUTUMN THROUGH TO SPRING

51 SPRING IN A SPANISH SAUCER

The yellow centres of the primroses combine beautifully with these dainty daffodils which are only just coming into flower. The Spanish saucer was kept in an unheated porch through the Winter and early Spring which explains why the daffodils are slightly taller than usual.

Site
Any aspect; could be enjoyed all Winter in an unheated porch.

Container
Large terracotta saucer shaped pot: 35cm (14″) in diameter, 15cm (6″) deep.

Plant
Early September to mid October.

In flower
The primroses will be in flower at the time of planting and should continue to flower in all but the worst Winter weather. The daffodils will bloom in the middle of April.

Ingredients
15 dwarf, multiheaded yellow daffodils *Narcissus* ‘Pencrebar’.
 5 pink primroses *Primula vulgaris.*
12 litres John Innes No 2 soil.
Drainage material such as grit or small pieces of polystyrene.

Method
1. Cover the base of the container with 2½cm (1″) drainage material and add 5cm (2″) soil.
2. Place the five primroses around the outside of the saucer.
3. Place the daffodil bulbs in the centre, making as wide a grouping as possible so that the bulbs are not touching.
4. Cover the bulbs with soil, and carefully fill in with soil around each primrose.
5. Water well. Add more soil to bring the level to within 2½cm (1″) of the rim.

Aftercare
Maintain the soil moisture throughout the Autumn, Winter and particularly in the Spring, but never water in frosty conditions.
    After the bulbs have finished flowering they may be planted out in the garden. However, make sure that they do not dry out until the leaves die down naturally in June or July.
    The primroses can be lifted from the container and planted out in a shady part of the garden.

52 A CHIMNEY POT AT THE FRONT DOOR

In Autumn, the warm tones of the cyclamen provide a perfect match for the front door. In Spring, the picture is transformed by pale yellow daffodils and pale blue pansies. The ingredients given below are for just one pot.

Site
Sheltered position by the front door; any aspect.

Container
Plastic or terracotta pot to fit inside the top of the actual chimney pot. Choose one as large as possible but make sure it doesn't sit too proud. This one is 30cm (12″) in diameter, and 22½cm (9″) deep.

Plant
September or early October, and again in early Spring.

In flower
The cyclamen should flower until the first sharp frost; in London this may be as late as Christmas. Replace them with pansies in early Spring so that they form a lovely display with the narcissi at the end of March.

Ingredients
  2 red pot plant cyclamen *Cyclamen persicum* 'Perfection Mixed': choose one with erect foliage and plenty of flower buds.
  2 long variegated ivies *Hedera helix* 'Chester' or 'Eva'.
  1 variegated shrub such as *Hebe* x *andersonii* 'Variegata', a tender hybrid which should survive most Winters, although not all. Choose one with plenty of flower spikes.
24 dwarf yellow daffodils *Narcissus cyclamineus* 'February Silver'.
  2 early pale blue pansies to replace the cyclamen *Viola* x *wittrockiana* F1 hybrid.
16 litres John Innes No 2 soil.
Drainage material such as grit or small pieces of polystyrene.

Method
  1. Cover the base of the container with 2½cm (1″) drainage material and add 7½cm (3″) soil.
  2. Place the ivies at the front of the container.
  3. Plant the daffodil bulbs in two layers behind the ivies, leaving a small gap in the centre.
  4. Cover the bulbs with soil until just their tips show.
  5. Place the hebe in the centre gap so that it does not sit on any of the bulbs.
  6. Plant two empty flower pots either side of the hebe.
  7. Add more soil so that the level is raised to within 2½cm (1″) of the rim.
  8. Water well and add more soil to regain the former level.
  9. Remove the flower pots and plant the cyclamen with their roots tucked well down into the soil.
10. Lift the pot and place it carefully in the chimney pot.
11. Arrange the ivy trails attractively down the front.

Aftercare
Check that the soil remains moist throughout the Autumn, but never water the cyclamen directly as their needs are less than average, and never water the pot at all in frosty conditions.

After the cyclamen have been caught by the frost remove them from the container and, in early Spring, replace them with the pansies. When the bulbs have finished flowering they may be planted out in the garden. Make sure, however, that they do not dry out until the leaves die down naturally in June or July.

You may like to keep the ivy for a Summer display. The hebe should be pruned before being moved back to the garden: cut it back to within 7½cm (3″) of the base to encourage it to make new shoots and remain bushy around the bottom. By the Autumn it should be ready for another display in a container.

53 AUTUMN GLORY, SPRING CHARM

Again the same basic planting can create a wonderful picture in both Autumn and Spring. The greenery and bulbs remain all Winter; only the cyclamen disappear, to be replaced by pink primroses.

Site
Ideal for a town basement, or sheltered terrace; any aspect.

Container
Terracotta pedestal and bowl. Pedestal: 52½cm (21″) high; bowl: 52½cm (21″) in diameter, 20cm (8″) deep.

Plant
Early September to mid October.

In flower
The cyclamen will flower from the time of planting until the first sharp frost. Mild frosts may make the plants flop – don't despair, they may recover and last until Christmas, as these did. You will need to replace them by primroses in early Spring, after which the scillas will begin to flower. The display should be at its best in mid April.

Ingredients
1 large upright heather, at least 30cm (12″) high *Erica arborea* 'Albert's Gold'.
2 variegated shrubs 25½cm (10″) high *Hebe x andersonii* 'Variegata'; choose ones with plenty of flower buds.
2 variegated ivies *Hedera helix* 'Sagittifolia Variegata'.
10 white daffodils *Narcissus triandrus* 'Thalia'.
4 white bedding hyacinths *Hyacinthus orientalis* 'L'Innocence'.
25 blue scillas or squills *Scilla sibirica* 'Spring Beauty'.
4 pink pot-plant cyclamen *Cyclamen persicum* 'Perfection Mixed'; choose ones with erect sturdy foliage and with plenty of flower buds underneath.
4 pink primroses *Primula vulgaris*.
30 litres John Innes No 2 soil.
Drainage material such as small pieces of polystyrene.

Method
1. Cover the base of the container with 2½cm (1″) drainage material and add 5cm (2″) soil.

2. Plant the hebes to the centre right and centre left of the bowl.
3. Plant the heather immediately behind them.
4. Plant the two ivies so that they trail over the rim of the bowl on either side of the hebes.
5. Plant four empty pots, one behind the heather, one between each hebe and ivy, and the fourth near the front rim of the bowl, to mark the position of the four cyclamen.
6. Plant the daffodil bulbs in a narrow arc around the back and sides of the heather and between the hebes.
7. Plant the four hyacinth bulbs to form an arc around the front of the bowl, one on either side of the centre front pot, and one behind each hebe, quite close to the rim.
8. Firm the bulbs gently into the soil, and lightly cover with more soil until just the tips of the bulbs are showing.
9. Plant the scillas all around the bowl, mainly concentrating on the outer area. Firm them down gently and bring the soil to within 2½cm (1″) of the container rim.
10. Make sure the container looks well balanced and that all the plants are firmly in place, filling any remaining gaps with soil.
11. Water well. Add more soil if necessary to return the level to within 2½cm (1″) of the rim.
12. Remove the empty pots and plant the cyclamen, taking care that their roots sit well down in the container.

Aftercare
Maintain the soil moisture throughout the Autumn and Winter, but avoid direct watering on the cyclamen as their needs are well below average. Never water the container in frosty conditions.

When the cyclamen have been hit by the frost, remove them, and replace in early Spring with four pink primroses. After the bulbs have finished flowering they may be planted out in the garden. Make sure, however, that they have adequate moisture until the leaves die down naturally in June or July.

The hebes may be used for another display in the Autumn, and, like the bulbs, they can be lifted from the container and planted out in the garden. First trim the hebes. Cut them back severely to within 7½cm (3″) of the base to encourage the plants to make new shoots and remain bushy around the bottom. The heather and the ivies may be replanted in the container as part of a Summer display.

54 AUTUMN CHEER, SPRING PLEASURE

You don't have to go outside to enjoy these cyclamen and hebes throughout the Autumn – you can enjoy them from the comfort of your sitting room.

Site
Window ledge; some sun.

Container
Large wooden window box: 82½cm (33″) long, 20cm (8″) wide, 20cm (8″) deep.

Plant
Early October and early Spring.

In flower
The cyclamen will flower until the first sharp frost; in London this may be as late as Christmas. Then in early Spring plant the polyanthus and little pansies and enjoy a lovely display culminating with the tulip blooms in mid April.

Ingredients
3 red pot-plant cyclamen *Cyclamen persicum* 'Perfection Mixed'; look for ones with sturdy foliage and lots of flower buds underneath.
2 variegated shrubs such as hebes *Hebe* x *andersonii* 'Variegata'. Choose ones with flower spikes if possible, as the lavender flowers are very pretty.
12 red short mid season tulips *Tulipa greigii* 'Oriental Beauty'.
3 tall yellow polyanthus.
1 strip of viola or little pansies *Viola tricolor* 'Johnny Jump-Up'.
25 litres John Innes No 2 soil.
Drainage material, such as crocks, grit or small pieces of polystyrene.

Method
1. Cover the base of the container with 2½cm (1″) drainage material and add 5cm (2″) soil.
2. Plant the hebes, one either side of the centre.
3. Space the tulip bulbs along the front and back of the box, saving one for the middle of each end.
4. Cover with soil until just the tips show.
5. Plant three empty flower pots: one in the centre and one at each end to mark the position of the cyclamen.
6. Add more soil to bring level to within 2½cm (1″) of the rim of the box. Make sure the hebes are firmly in place.

7. Water well. Use extra soil if necessary to bring the level back to within 2½cm (1″) of the rim.
8. Now remove the three pots and plant the cyclamen, making sure that the roots are tucked down well into the soil.

Aftercare
Check that the soil remains moist throughout the Autumn, but never water the cyclamen directly, as their needs are less than average, and never water in frosty conditions.

Severe frost will kill the cyclamen; remove them from the box when they are dead.

Replace the cyclamen with the polyanthus in early Spring. At the same time, carefully remove the violas from their polystyrene surround and separate the plants. Space them along both the front and back edges of the box so that they can be enjoyed equally from both inside and outside the house.

After flowering, the tulips may be planted in a sunny part of the garden. Make sure, however, that they do not dry out until the leaves die down naturally in June or July, and be warned – they may only flower spasmodically next season.

The polyanthus and hebes may be used for another display in the Autumn, and they too may be planted out in the garden. Prune the hebes by cutting them back severely to within 7½cm (3″) of the base to encourage the plant to make new shoots and remain bushy around the bottom.

The violas may be planted out in the garden as well where they should continue flowering all Summer, particularly if they have been given some liquid feed.

55 WHITE FOR AUTUMN AND SPRING

This all-white Autumn display makes a wonderful picture framed by the smart white front to the house. By mid Spring the underplanting of the white daffodils is in full bloom, and blue and white cineraria have replaced the cyclamen.

Site
Window ledge; any aspect.

Container
Large terracotta window box: 80cm (32″) long, 20cm (8″) wide, 17½cm (7″) deep.

Plant
Early September to mid October.

In flower
The cyclamen should flower from the time of planting until the first sharp frost, which in London could be as late as December. The cineraria should be available from early April and will flower until the end of May. The daffodils will flower in mid April.

Ingredients
20 white daffodils *Narcissus triandrus* 'Thalia'.
 3 large white pot-plant cyclamen *Cyclamen persicum* 'Perfection Mixed'; choose ones with erect sturdy foliage and plenty of flower buds underneath.
 3 blue and white pot plant cinerarias *Senecio x hybridus (Cineraria cruenta)*; look for compact plants with lots of buds.
 2 silver leaved ivies *Hedera helix* 'Jubilee'.
25 litres John Innes No 2 soil.
Drainage material, such as crocks, grit, or small pieces of polystyrene.

Method
1. Cover the base of the container with 2½cm (1″) drainage material and add 5cm (2″) soil.
2. Plant the ivies at the front of the box, on either side of the centre.
3. Plant the daffodil bulbs in two groups behind the ivies.
4. Cover the bulbs with soil until just the tips show.

5. Plant three empty plant pots to mark the position of the cyclamen, one in the centre and one at each end of the box.
6. Add more soil so that the level is raised to within 2½cm (1″) of the rim.
7. Water well and add more soil to regain the former level.
8. Remove the plant pots and plant the cyclamen so that their roots are tucked well down into the soil.

Aftercare
Check that the soil remains moist throughout the Autumn, but never water the cyclamen directly as their needs are less than average. Avoid watering in frosty weather.

After the cyclamen have been caught by the frost remove them from the container. In early April, or when the weather warms up, replace them with cineraria. They will continue flowering until the end of May, after which they should be discarded.

By the end of May the daffodils will long since have finished flowering; deadhead them to neaten their appearance while the cineraria display still lasts, but when this is over plant them out in the garden. However, make sure that they do not dry out until the leaves die down naturally in June or July.

The ivies may be used for another display in the Autumn and can be planted out in the garden as well.

56 AUTUMN BERRIES FOLLOWED BY HYACINTHS

This time the Autumn colour is provided by the rich tones of the solanum berries. In Spring we see an unusual combination of hyacinths.

Site
Sheltered balcony or terrace, any aspect.

Container
Terracotta pedestal and bowl. Pedestal: 52½cm (21″) high. Bowl: 52½cm (21″) in diameter, 20cm (8″) high.

Plant
Early September to early October.

In flower
The berries should remain until Christmas, depending on the birds and severe frosts; the bulbs will bloom in mid April and the little pansies will flower from early Spring onwards.

Ingredients
1 large upright heather, at least 30cm (12″) high *Erica arborea* 'Albert's Gold'.
3 pot-plant solanums or Winter cherries *Solanum capsicastrum* 'Covent Garden', 30cm (12″) high.
3 variegated ivies *Hedera helix* 'Goldchild', 'Chicago Variegated' or 'Heise'.
7 bedding hyacinths of which 4 *Hyacinthus orientalis* 'Gypsy Queen' (salmon pink), 3 *Hyacinthus orientalis* 'Blue Magic' (deep blue).
3 white Roman hyacinths *Hyacinthus orientalis albulus* 'Snow White', with several dainty flower spikes from each bulb.
2 strips or 6 pots of violas (tricolor and yellow) *Viola tricolor* 'Johnny Jump-Up' and 'Prince John' 15cm (6″) high.
1 salmon pink or pale yellow primrose *Primula vulgaris*.
30 litres John Innes No 2 soil.
Drainage material, such as grit, small stones, crocks or small pieces of polystyrene.

Method
1. Cover the base of the container with 2½cm (1″) drainage material and add 5cm (2″) soil.
2. Position the heather in the centre of the container.
3. Plant one ivy at the front, and one on either side of the heather so that they trail over the rim.
4. Plant the three solanums close to the rim; one behind the heather and one between each ivy.
5. Plant the 'Gypsy Queen' hyacinths in an arc between the heather and the front solanums. Plant the three 'Blue Magic' hyacinths around the heather, forming a triangle with the apex at the back between the heather and the solanum.
6. Plant the three 'Snow White' hyacinths to echo the arc of the 'Gypsy Queens', but nearer the rim.
7. Cover the bulbs with soil, bringing the level to within 2½cm (1″) of the rim.
8. Make sure the container looks well-balanced and that all the plants are firmly in place, filling any remaining gaps with soil.
9. Water well. Add more soil if necessary to bring the level back to within 2½cm (1″) of the rim.

Aftercare
Maintain soil moisture throughout the Autumn, Winter and particularly in the Spring, but never water in frosty conditions. The solanums are thirsty plants and will soon let you know by their drooping leaves if they need more water.

By mid Winter the solanum berries will have shrivelled and be unsightly; remove the plants from the pot, top up empty holes with soil and transfer the solanums to the garden.

In early Spring plant the new primrose behind the front ivy. Plant the violas in the gaps left by the solanums and also around the rim of the container to form a pretty frill.

When the bulbs have finished flowering, replant all the contents in the garden unless you wish to retain the ivy and the heather for a Summer display. The violas should continue to flower throughout the Summer.

57 A POT TO LAST ALL WINTER

These colourful pansies flowered all through the Autumn, and then survived one of the worst Winters on record, and were still flowering happily the following May. They are very good value indeed and so easy to look after.

Site
Any aspect.

Container
Small terracotta pot: 15cm (6″) in diameter, 20cm (8″) deep.

Plant
Early September to mid October.

In flower
From time of planting until next Summer, although severe Winter weather will stop the flowering for a while.

Ingredients
3 Winter pansies (yellows and clarets make good partners) *Viola* x *wittrockiana* 'Universal'.
1 variegated ivy *Hedera helix* 'Goldchild'.
3 litres John Innes No 2 soil.
Drainage material such as grit, crocks or small pieces polystyrene.

Method
1. Cover the base of the container with 2½cm (1″) drainage material and add 7½cm (3″) soil.
2. Position the ivy at the front of the pot so that it trails over the edge.
3. Plant the pansies around the ivy.
4. Fill in the gaps with soil and make sure that the container looks well balanced and that all the plants are firmly in place.
5. Water well. Add more soil if necessary to bring the level to within 2½cm (1″) of the rim.

Aftercare
Maintain soil moisture throughout the Autumn, Winter and Spring, but never water in frosty conditions. Pansies are thirsty drinkers and will soon flag if they are dry. Feed regularly throughout their flowering period with a liquid plant feed according to the instructions on the packet.

Deadhead the flowers to encourage them to produce even more and discard when they have eventually finished blooming.

58 WINTER FOLIAGE WITH A HINT OF SPRING

The plants in this container are five years old and it is now predominately a foliage box. It maintains its interest throughout the Winter with its central conifer, its golden leaved euonymus, and its trailing ivies. It can still have a seasonal look, however, and here it is fronted by cheerful yellow crocuses followed, in April, by creamy daffodils.

Site
Window ledge, any aspect.

Container
Medium terracotta window box: 45cm (18″) long, 20cm (8″) wide, 15cm (6″) high.

Plant
Early September to mid October.

In flower
Mid March to early April.

Ingredients
10 dwarf daffodils *Narcissus jonquilla* 'Waterperry'; these are scented and some will be multiheaded.
10 yellow crocus, each will produce several flowers *Crocus aureus* 'Dutch Yellow'.
 1 slow growing conifer such as a dwarf Lawson cypress *Chamaecyparis lawsoniana* 'Ellwoodii'.
 2 trailing ivies *Hedera helix* 'Chicago'.
 2 variegated shrubs *Euonymus japonicus* 'Aureopictus'.
10 litres John Innes No 2 soil.
Drainage material such as small pieces of polystyrene.

Method
1. Assuming you are starting entirely from scratch, cover the base of the container with 2½cm (1″) drainage material and add 5cm (2″) soil. If you already have an established foliage window box remove all the plants, and follow the instructions as given, substituting your own foliage plants. This is a good opportunity to change the soil and to trim the ivies.
2. Plant the chamaecyparis in the centre, and the euonymus at either end of the box.
3. Plant the ivies at either side of the centre and trail over the front.
4. Place two daffodil bulbs in each corner of the box and three on either side of the chamaecyparis.
5. Cover the bulbs with soil until just the tips show.
6. Now plant the crocus corms along the front and

at the sides of the box. Cover them with soil.
7. Make sure the container looks well balanced and that all the plants are firmly in place, and fill any remaining gaps with soil.
8. Water well. Add more soil if necessary to bring the level to within 2½cm (1″) of the rim.

Aftercare
The plants in the box are so well developed that they will be very thirsty. Great care must be taken to maintain soil moisture throughout the Autumn, Winter and particularly in the Spring. However, never water in frosty conditions.

After the bulbs have finished flowering they may be planted out in the garden, but make sure that they do not dry out until the leaves die down naturally in June or July. The rest of the plants may be used for another display in the Summer. (See Recipe 125, page 154.)

Now is the time to prune the ivies and euonymus. Trim them back well to maintain a good shape and to encourage bushy growth.

59 A CONIFER BARREL WITH TULIPS AND HYACINTHS

You often see a wooden barrel with just a conifer stuck in the middle. Well, here's the conifer surrounded by brilliant red tulips and fragrant hyacinths. A welcome sight indeed.

Site
A little sun certainly helps.

Container
A large wooden half barrel: 55cm (22″) in diameter, 37½cm (15″) deep.

Plant
October.

In flower
Mid April.

Ingredients
6 white bedding hyacinths *Hyacinthus orientalis* 'L'Innocence'.
15 early red tulips *Tulipa kaufmanniana* 'Alfred Cortot' with its lovely markings on the leaves.
1 slow-growing conifer *Chamaecyparis lawsoniana* 'Ellwoodii'; this dwarf Lawson cypress has been in the barrel for ten years.
A small quantity of John Innes No 2 soil.

Method
We will assume you already have a container with a large established conifer or a small tree in the centre. As you would find it hard work to uproot the tree each time you wished to do a new planting around the edge you should start from the surface and work down.

1. Take a sharp trowel and measuring from the top of the barrel, dig a 20cm (8″) deep, 10cm (4″) wide trench around the tree. It should be about 5–15cm (2″–6″) in from the edge of the barrel.
2. Plant the hyacinth bulbs at regular intervals at the bottom of the trench towards the outside edge of the barrel.
3. Fill the bottom of the trench with soil until just the tips of the bulbs show.
4. Now plant the tulip bulbs; six in between the hyacinths and nine forming an inner circle in the trench.
5. Cover the bulbs with soil.
6. Often the soil level in a barrel is allowed to sink quite low. If this is the case here, use this opportunity to correct it. Add some John Innes No 2 so that the level is brought within 2½cm (1″) of the rim.
7. Water well.

Aftercare
Maintain the soil moisture throughout the Autumn, Winter and particularly in the Spring, but never water in frosty conditions.

After the bulbs have finished flowering they may be removed. Their roots will have grown right to the bottom of the barrel and you may have difficulty in getting them all out. Do it as carefully and as well as you can to minimise damage either to the tree or to the bulbs. If you don't manage to get the roots out as well as the bulb you might as well throw them away.

Replant the bulbs in the garden, the tulips in a sunny spot. But be warned, the tulip flowers may not be as good next year.

60 ANOTHER CONIFER BARREL

Here is another conifer barrel, slightly bigger than the last. It had colourful solanums around the base in the Autumn. In Spring it is transformed by the delicate salmon-pink hyacinths and the peachy-yellow trumpets of the daffodils.

Site
Any aspect.

Container
Large wooden half barrel; 60cm (24″) in diameter, 37½cm (15″) deep.

Plant
September to October.

In flower
The solanum berries will be colourful from the time of planting until Christmas, depending on the birds and severe frosts. The bulbs will bloom from early to mid April.

Ingredients
3 pot plant solanums or Winter cherries *Solanum capsicastrum* 'Covent Garden', 30cm (12″) high.
8 bedding hyacinths *Hyacinthus orientalis* 'Gypsy Queen'.
20 cream daffodils with peach-yellow trumpets *Narcissus* 'Salome'.
1 slow-growing conifer *Chaemaecyparis lawsoniana* 'Ellwoodii'; this dwarf Lawson cypress has been in the barrel for ten years.
A small amount of John Innes No 2 soil.

Method
Again we will assume you already have a container with a large established conifer like this *Chamaecyparis lawsoniana* 'Ellwoodii' or a small tree such as a box or bay in the middle.
1. Take a sharp trowel and, measuring from the top of the barrel, dig a 20cm (8″) deep, 10cm (4″) wide trench around the tree. It should be about 5–15cm (2–6″) from the edge of the barrel.
2. Plant the hyacinth bulbs at regular intervals at the bottom of the trench towards the outside edge of the barrel.
3. Fill the bottom of the trench with the soil you have just taken out until just the tips show.
4. Now plant the daffodil bulbs, eight between the hyacinths, the rest around the centre.
5. Cover with more of the same soil.

6. Add some John Innes No 2 soil so that the level is brought within 2½cm (1″) of the rim.
7. The solanums should now be planted around the front of the barrel.
8. Water well. Add more soil if necessary to regain the former level.

Aftercare
Maintain soil moisture throughout the Autumn, Winter and particularly in the Spring. The solanums are thirsty plants and soon let you know by their drooping leaves that they need more water, but never water in frosty conditions.

By mid Winter the solanum berries will have shrivelled so remove them from the barrel and plant them in a sheltered part of the garden where they can flower and berry again next season.

After the bulbs have finished flowering they too may be planted out in the garden. Take care, however, to remove the bulbs with their stems, leaves and roots intact.

Make sure that the bulbs do not dry out until the leaves die down naturally in June or July.

61 SPRING FEVER IN A HANGING BASKET

Bulbs never trail, but don't let that stop you trying to create a lovely hanging basket which will give great pleasure both in Autumn and Winter and then burst into full colour in early Spring. With the help of the ivies and primroses to soften the rim of the basket, and two Winter flowering heathers to form the frame, you have an ideal background to show off some of your favourite dwarf bulbs.

Site
Ideal for hanging at the front door where it can be enjoyed to the utmost. Let the basket hang at eye level so that all the plants can be fully appreciated. Any aspect, but some sun helps.

Container
Wire hanging basket: 35cm (14″) in diameter, with a strong 27½cm (11″) bracket.

Plant
Early September to early October.

In flower
The primroses will be in bloom at the time of planting although cold Winter weather may halt their flowering until Spring. The heathers will be a cascade of white from late Winter onwards, lasting for the entire bulb display which will start in mid March and continue well into April.

Ingredients
1 hardy shrub to add central height *Euonymus japonicus* 'Aureopictus'; 30cm (12″) high.
2 white heathers with spreading habit *Erica herbacea* (*E. carnea*) 'Springwood White'.
2 primroses, *Primula vulgaris*; one yellow and one brick orange.
1 variegated ivy *Hedera helix* 'Glacier'.
10 multiheaded dwarf yellow daffodils *Narcissus cyclamineus* 'Tête à Tête'.
10 mixed yellow and purple crocuses *Crocus aureus* 'Dutch Yellow' and *Crocus vernus* 'Purpureus Grandiflorus'.
6 early dwarf tulips *Tulipa kaufmanniana* 'Shakespeare'.
10 litres John Innes No 2 soil.
A basketful of moss: sphagnum preferably, or ordinary wreath moss from a florists shop.
A circle of plastic sheeting the size of a dinner plate, cut from a plastic bag.

Method
1. Line the basket with a generous thickness of moss, starting at the base and bringing it well up the sides so that you form a collar above the rim of the basket.
2. Cut four 2½cm (1″) slits in the plastic circle and place over the moss lining in the bottom of the basket.
3. Cover the plastic circle with 2½cm (1″) soil.
4. Place the euonymus at the back of the basket.
5. Place the heathers on either side of the euonymus so that they spread over the rim of the basket.
6. Place the ivy at the front of the basket so that it trails over the side and down the front.
7. Plant the primroses to the right and left of the ivy so that they add Winter colour to the front of the basket, as well as softening the rim.
8. Plant the tulip bulbs between the euonymus and the heathers at the back of the basket.
9. Plant the daffodil bulbs in a broad group in the centre of the basket coming slightly forward between the primroses and the ivies.
10. Cover with soil until just the tips show.
11. Take the purple crocus corms and form a centre line from amongst the daffodils to the front rim between the ivy and one of the primroses.
12. Take the yellow crocus corms and plant around the heathers, leaving one for tucking into the centre front.
13. Make sure the container looks well balanced and that all the plants and bulbs are firmly in place, filling any remaining gaps with soil.
14. Water well. Add more soil to bring the level to within 2½cm (1″) of the rim.

Aftercare
Maintain soil moisture throughout the Autumn, Winter and particularly in the Spring, but never water in frosty conditions.

After the bulbs have finished flowering they may be planted out in the garden. However, make sure that they do not dry out until the leaves die down naturally in June or July. The rest of the plants may be used for another display in the Autumn, and like the bulbs they can be planted out in the garden.

The heathers should be planted in an open position with lots of peat mixed in the soil beneath them. The primroses appreciate a moist site; the euonymus and ivy are not fussy.

62 JUST FOR AUTUMN

Plant this Autumn arrangement by your front door and enjoy an unusual combination of colours every time you come home.

Site
Close to the house, as sheltered as possible.

Container
Pedestal and urn. Urn: 30cm (12″) in diameter, 22½cm (9″) deep. Pedestal: 42½cm (17″) high.

Plant
Early September to early October.

In flower
From time of planting until first sharp frost: in London, this could be as late as Christmas.

Ingredients
1 variegated shrub such as *Hebe* x *andersonii* 'Variegata'; choose one with plenty of flower spikes.
1 *Hebe* 'La Seduisante', with dark green leaves and violet blue flowers.
1 solanum or Winter cherry *Solanum capsicastrum* 'Covent Garden'; 30cm (12″) high with lots of green or orange berries.
1 white pot plant cyclamen *Cyclamen persicum* 'Perfection Mixed': choose one with erect foliage and plenty of flower buds.
16 litres John Innes No 2 soil.
Drainage material such as grit, or small pieces of polystyrene.

Method
1. Cover the base of the container with 2½cm (1″) drainage material and add 10cm (4″) soil.
2. Plant the 'La Seduisante' hebe at the centre back, the variegated hebe to centre left, and the solanum to the centre right.
3. Make sure the container looks well balanced and that all the plants are firmly in place.
4. Plant an empty plant pot in the centre front position and fill in all the gaps with soil.
5. Water well. Add more soil if necessary to bring the level to within 2½cm (1″) of the rim.
6. Remove the empty pot and plant the cyclamen.

Aftercare
Maintain soil moisture throughout the Autumn but be aware that the needs of the hebes and solanum are much greater than that of the cyclamen. Never water in frosty conditions.

It is likely that the cyclamen and then the solanum will die if there is a very sharp frost, although they will withstand much colder conditions than is generally supposed.

The rest of the plants should survive all but the worst Winters. You may choose to keep them in the container as part of a Spring display, replacing the cyclamen and solanum with a primrose and perhaps a pot of growing dwarf daffodils. After these have finished flowering remove all the contents to the garden.

If you wish to use the hebes for another display in the Autumn, now is the time to prune them. Cut them back severely to within 7½cm (3″) of the base to encourage the plant to make new shoots and remain bushy around the bottom.

63 FIRE IN A CHIMNEY POT

Here is a very tall chimney pot sitting in a London basement. The pansies were in flower throughout the Autumn and Winter, except in all but the worst weather. In Spring they are joined by fiery red tulips.

Site
Any aspect, although prefers some sun.

Container
Small plastic or terracotta container to fit inside the top of the chimney pot. Choose one as large as possible but make sure it doesn't sit too proud in the chimney pot. This one is 25cm (10″) in diameter. The actual chimney pot can be any size, although remember that the big ones are extremely heavy to move.

Plant
Early October to mid November

In flower
The yellow pansies should flower throughout the Winter, except in the coldest spells. The tulips will bloom in early April.

Ingredients
20 multiheaded red tulips *Tulipa praestans* 'Tubergen's Variety'.
2 yellow Winter flowering pansies *Viola* x *wittrockiana* 'Universal'.
1 variegated ivy *Hedera helix* 'Harald'.
10 litres John Innes No 2 soil.
Drainage material such as grit or small pieces of polystyrene.

Method
1. Cover the base of the inner container with 2½cm (1″) drainage material and add 5cm (2″) soil.
2. Position the ivy at the front of the container.
3. Plant ten tulip bulbs at the base of the container, behind the ivy.
4. Cover with soil until just their tips show.
5. Now make a double layer with the other ten bulbs, planting them in between the tips of the bottom layer.
6. Add more soil so that the bulbs are completely covered.

7. Plant the two pansies on either side of the ivy. Here they appear only on one side but they have both been drawn towards the sun.
8. Make sure that all the plants are firmly in place, filling any remaining gaps with soil.
9. Water well. Add more soil if necessary to bring the level to within 2½cm (1″) of the rim.
10. Lift the pot and place it carefully in the chimney pot.

Aftercare
Maintain soil moisture throughout the Autumn, Winter and particularly in the Spring, but never water in frosty conditions. Pansies are thirsty drinkers and will soon flag if lacking

The pansies should be deadheaded regularly and be given a liquid feed from early Spring onwards.

After the bulbs have finished flowering they may be planted out in a sunny part of the garden. However, make sure that they do not dry out until the leaves die down naturally in June or July.

Discard the pansies, but replant the ivy ready for another display in the Summer.

Spring Window Boxes

64 SIMPLICITY IN EARLY SPRING

This display is one of the easiest to plant and is sure to give several weeks of lovely fresh colour. The large white flowers of the crocus will open towards the end of March joined by the graceful blooms of 'February Gold'.

Site
Window ledge, with some sun.

Container
Medium terracotta window box: 45cm (18″) long, 17½cm (7″) wide, 17½cm (7″) deep.

Plant
Early September to early October.

In flower
Towards the end of March through to early April.

Ingredients
10 early dwarf daffodils *Narcissus cyclamineus* 'February Gold'.
20 Dutch white crocuses *Crocus vernus* 'Jeanne D'Arc'.
 2 variegated ivies *Hedera helix* 'Kolibri'. This has a lot of white in its variegation but any variegated ivy would be attractive.
12 litres of John Innes No 2 soil.
Drainage material such as grit or small pieces of polystyrene.

Method
1. Cover the base of the container with 2½cm (1″) of drainage material and add 5cm (2″) soil.
2. Position the ivies at the two front corners of the box.
3. Place the daffodil bulbs in two rows towards the back of the box, avoiding contact either with each other or with the side of the container.

4. Cover the bulbs with soil until just the tips are showing.
5. Now place the crocus corms around the daffodil bulbs and along the front of the box. Firm them gently into the soil.
6. Top up with more soil to bring the level to within 2½cm (1″) of the rim.
7. Water well, adding more soil as is necessary to regain the former level.

Aftercare
Maintain soil moisture throughout the Autumn, Winter and particularly in the Spring, but never water in frosty conditions.

After the crocuses and daffodils have finished flowering they may be planted out in the garden: take care, however, to minimize root disturbance and make sure that they do not dry out until the leaves die down naturally in June or July.

The ivies may be used for another display in the Autumn, and may also be planted out in the garden.

65 A BOX OF PRIMROSES

This display includes two kinds of daffodil, one flowering slightly earlier than the other so that they fully complement the long flowering period of the primroses. The pale yellows make a delightful colour combination with the pretty blue of the scillas.

Site
Window ledge, any aspect.

Container
Medium plastic window box: 60cm (24″) long, 15cm (6″) wide, 15cm (6″) deep.

Plant
Early September to October.

In flower
End March to early April.

Ingredients
14 pale yellow daffodils, of which
 8 *Narcissus cyclamineus* 'February Silver'; its trumpet fades to pale cream as it ages.
 6 *Narcissus jonquilla* 'Waterperry'; this is multiheaded, scented and grows taller as it matures.
12 blue scilla or squills *Scilla sibirica* 'Spring Beauty', with several flower spikes from each bulb.
 2 primroses *Primula vulgaris*.
11 litres John Innes No 2 soil.
Drainage material such as small pieces of polystyrene.

Method
1. Cover the base of the container with 2½cm (1″) drainage material and add 5cm (2″) soil.
2. Plant the two primroses on either side of the centre.
3. Plant the 'February Silver' bulbs along the back of the box.
4. Plant the 'Waterperry' bulbs in two groups in the middle of the box close to the primroses.
5. Cover the bulbs with soil until just the tips show.
6. Now plant the scilla bulbs between the two primroses and at either end of the box, then cover with soil.
7. Make sure that the primroses are firmly in place, filling any remaining gaps with soil.
8. Water well. Add more soil if necessary to bring the level to within 2½cm (1″) of the rim.

Aftercare
Maintain soil moisture throughout the Autumn, Winter and particularly in the Spring, but never water in frosty conditions.

After the bulbs have finished flowering they may be planted out in the garden; however, make sure that they do not dry out until the leaves die down naturally in June or July.

The primroses may be used for another display in the Autumn, and like the bulbs they can be lifted from the box and planted out in a moist area in the garden. Eventually you may wish to divide them but you may find large clumps attractive.

66 ROMAN HYACINTHS AND TULIPS

This is a striking combination of red 'Stockholm' tulips, white Roman hyacinths and dark green ivies.

Site
Window ledge, some sun.

Container
Large wooden window box (painted white): 80cm (32″) long, 20cm (8″) wide, 17½cm (7″) deep.

Plant
Early October to mid November.

In flower
Early to mid April.

Ingredients
12 double early tulips *Tulipa* 'Stockholm'.
 6 white Roman hyacinths *Hyacinthus orientalis albulus* 'Snow White'.
 3 ivies *Hedera helix* 'Ivalace'.
25 litres John Innes No 2 soil.
Drainage material such as small pieces of poly-styrene.

Method
1. Cover the base of the container with 2½cm (1″) drainage material and add 5cm (2″) soil.
2. Plant the three ivies at the front of the box, one in the centre and one at each end.
3. Plant four Roman hyacinths along the front of the box between the ivies. Plant the other two in the middle of the box either side of the centre.
4. Plant the tulip bulbs around the hyacinths so that an even display is achieved.
5. Cover the bulbs with soil. Make sure the container looks well balanced and that the ivies are firmly in place.
6. Fill any remaining gaps with soil, bringing the level to within 2½cm (1″) of the rim. Water well. Add more soil if necessary to regain the former level.

Aftercare
Maintain soil moisture throughout the Autumn, Winter and particularly in the Spring, but never water in frosty conditions.

After the bulbs have finished flowering they may be planted out in the garden; however, make sure that they do not dry out until the leaves die down naturally in June or July.

The ivies may be used for another display in the Autumn, and should be planted out in the garden.

67 FRAGRANT HYACINTHS

These pretty pink and dainty blue hyacinths make a charming picture underplanted with white arabis. Even better, they have a wonderful scent.

Site
Window ledge; partial shade.

Container
Large wooden window box (painted white): 80cm (32″) long, 20 cm (8″) wide, 17½cm (7″) deep.

Plant
Early September to mid October.

In flower
The arabis begins to flower in early March, joined by the hyacinths in early April.

Ingredients
5 pink Roman or multiflora hyacinths such as *Hyacinthus orientalis albulus* 'Rosalie'; otherwise use a pink bedding hyacinth such as 'Pink Pearl'.
5 blue Roman or multiflora hyacinths such as *Hyacinthus orientalis albulus* 'Blue Borah' with several flowering spikes to each bulb.
3 pots or 1 strip of *Arabis caucasica* 'Snowflake'.
25 litres John Innes No 2 soil.
Drainage material such as grit or small pieces of polystyrene.

Method
1. Cover the base of the container with 2½cm (1″) drainage material and add 5cm (2″) soil.
2. Plant the pink hyacinths along the middle of the box and the blue ones at the back, spacing them so that the blue ones will show through.
3. Cover the bulbs with soil until just the tips show.
4. Now plant the arabis along the front of the box; if you are using a strip of plants carefully separate them before planting.
5. Make sure that all the plants are firmly in place, add more soil to bring the level to within 2½cm (1″) of the rim.
6. Water well. Add more soil if necessary to regain the former level.

Aftercare
Maintain soil moisture throughout the Autumn, Winter and particularly in the Spring, but never water in frosty conditions.

After the bulbs have finished flowering they may be planted out in the garden; however, make sure that they do not dry out until the leaves die down naturally in June or July.

The arabis may be used for another display in the Autumn, and like the bulbs, can be lifted from the container and planted out in the garden. It likes well drained soil with partial shade and should be severely cut back to encourage a good shape.

68 SPRING CREAMS

Earlier in the Spring white crocuses filled the box; now it is adorned with creamy 'Waterperry' daffodils and soft blue hyacinths.

Site
Window ledge; any aspect, although sun brings out the best in the crocuses.

Container
Large terracotta window box: 80cm (32″) long, 20cm (8″) wide, 17½cm (7″) deep.

Plant
Early September to mid October.

In flower
End of March to mid April.

Ingredients
15 white crocuses *Crocus vernus* 'Jeanne D'Arc'.
24 dwarf daffodils *Narcissus jonquilla* 'Waterperry'.
 3 blue bedding hyacinths *Hyacinthus orientalis* 'Delft Blue'.
 2 ivies *Hedera helix* 'Sagittifolia', whose leaves turn a rich bronze in the Autumn; variegated ivies would also be attractive here.
25 litres John Innes No 2 soil.
Drainage material such as grit or small pieces of polystyrene.

Method
1. Cover the base of the container with 2½cm (1″) drainage material and add 5cm (2″) soil.
2. Arrange the ivies over the front of the box on either side of the centre.
3. Plant the hyacinth bulbs, one in the centre and one at each end.
4. Now plant the daffodil bulbs in two rows along the front and back of the box.
5. Cover the bulbs with soil until just their tips show.
6. Gently firm the crocus corms into the soil along the front of the box between the daffodil bulbs.
7. Make sure the ivies are firmly in place and bring the soil level to within 2½cm (1″) of the rim.
8. Water well. Add more soil if necessary to regain its former level.

Aftercare
Maintain soil moisture throughout the Autumn, Winter and particularly in the Spring, but never water in frosty conditions.

After the bulbs have finished flowering they may be planted out in the garden. Make sure, however, that they do not dry out until the leaves die down naturally in June or July.

The ivies may be used for another display in the Autumn, and like the bulbs they can be lifted from the container and planted out in the garden.

69 SPRING MELODY

This is a colourful combination of mid Spring flowers. It is particularly fragrant and will bloom over a long period.

Site
Window ledge, sunny aspect.

Container
Large terracotta window box: 80cm (32″) long, 20cm (8″) wide, 17½cm (7″) deep.

Plant
Early September to October.

In flower
Mid April until early May.

Ingredients

8 bedding hyacinths *Hyacinthus orientalis* 'Gipsy Queen' (an unusual salmon pink). This is an extravagant use of hyacinths but they do produce a delicious scent. You could halve the number.

12 dainty yellow daffodils *Narcissus* 'Pencrebar'.

3 primroses *Primula juliae* hybrid 'Wanda'; a good hardy variety which will last for years afterwards in the garden.

2 golden alyssums *Alyssum saxatile* 'Flore Pleno'.

25 litres John Innes No 2 soil.

Drainage material such as small pieces of polystyrene or horticultural grit.

Method

1. Cover the base of the container with 2½cm (1″) drainage material and add 5cm (2″) soil.
2. Place the primroses at the front of the box; one in the centre and one at each end.
3. Plant the alyssums between the primroses so that they will trail over the rim.
4. Now plant the hyacinth bulbs to form two arcs around the alyssums.
5. Plant the daffodil bulbs in the remaining free spaces, taking care to save at least four for the area around the centre primrose, and two for either end.
6. Cover all the bulbs with soil.
7. Make sure the container looks well balanced and that the plants are firmly in place, filling any remaing gaps with soil.
8. Water well. Add more soil if necessary to bring the level to within 2½cm (1″) of the rim.

Aftercare

Maintain soil moisture throughout the Autumn, Winter and particularly in the Spring, but never water in frosty conditions.

After the bulbs have finished flowering they may be planted out in the garden. Make sure, however, that they do not dry out until the leaves die down naturally in June or July. To minimize root disturbance you could plant them mixed together as they grew. However, if you wish to plant them separately be very careful how you part the roots. Both the daffodils and the hyacinths should bloom well for several years.

Now is the time to cut the alyssums back to encourage well shaped plants for next season. Find a sunny spot in the garden for their Summer home and you may be able to use them again in the Autumn.

The primroses are not so choosy where they live and by the Autumn will have made good growth. You may wish to divide them before replanting.

70 SOFTNESS AND SCENT

The three bulbs echo the pattern on the window box. The delicate colour of the hyacinths is enhanced by the dainty white arabis. The fragrance from the hyacinths is an additional attraction.

Site
Window ledge; any aspect.

Container
Small terracotta window box: 35cm (14″) long, 17½cm (7″) wide, 17½cm (7″) deep.

Plant
Early September to mid October.

In flower
The arabis should begin to flower in March; the hyacinths will bloom towards the middle of April.

Ingredients
  3 bedding hyacinths *Hyacinthus orientalis* 'Gypsy Queen'.
  2 white Spring rock plants *Arabis caucasica* 'Snow-flake'.
10 litres John Innes No 2 soil.
Drainage material such as small pieces of polystyrene.

Method
1. Cover the base of the container with 2½cm (1″) drainage material and add 5cm (2″) soil.
2. Space the three hyacinth bulbs along the middle of the box.
3. Cover the bulbs with soil until only the tips show.
4. Plant the two arabis plants between the hyacinth bulbs.
5. Firm them in, then top up with soil to within 2½cm (1″) of the rim.
6. Water well. Add more soil if necessary to bring the level back to within 2½cm (1″) of the rim.

Aftercare
Maintain the soil moisture throughout the Autumn, Winter and particularly in the Spring, but never water in frosty conditions.

After the bulbs have finished flowering they may be planted out in the garden. Make sure, however, that they do not dry out until the leaves die down naturally in June or July.

The arabis plants may be used for another display in the Autumn, and like the bulbs can be lifted from the container and planted out in the garden. They prefer partial shade. Cut them back severely after flowering to keep them tidy and encourage them to make new shoots. In the Autumn you may wish to divide them.

71 SIMPLE PINKS AND MAUVES

A simple planting with lovely pink tulips fronted by trailing aubrieta.

Site
Window ledge; sunny.

Container
Large plastic window box: 85cm (34″) long, 20cm (8″) wide, 17½cm (7″) deep.

Plant
Early October to mid November.

In flower
The aubrieta will start to flower in early Spring and continue for many weeks. The tulips will bloom from early to late April.

Ingredients
16 pink double early tulips *Tulipa* 'Peach Blossom'.
 3 mid season aubrieta *Aubrieta deltoidea* 'Blue Cascade'.
25 litres John Innes No 2 soil.
Drainage material such as small pieces of polystyrene.

Method
1. Cover the base of the container with 2½cm (1″) drainage material and add 5cm (2″) soil.
2. Plant the tulip bulbs in two rows along the length of the box.
3. Cover the bulbs with soil.
4. Plant the aubrietas at the front of the box; one at either end, and one in the centre.
5. Make sure the container looks well balanced and that all the plants are firmly in place, filling any remaining gaps with soil.
6. Water well. Add more soil if necessary to bring the level to within 2½cm (1″) of the rim.

Aftercare
Maintain soil moisture throughout the Autumn, Winter and particularly in the Spring, but never water in frosty conditions.

After the bulbs have finished flowering, lift them gently and plant out in a sunny part of the garden. Make sure, however, that they do not dry out until the leaves die down naturally in June or July. They may only bloom spasmodically next year.

The aubrietas may be used again in the Autumn, so plant them out in a sunny position in the garden. Cut them back well to encourage neat growth for the next season.

72 A LATE SPRING WINDOW BOX

Easy to plant and to look after, this display will last for a long time.

Site
Window ledge; any aspect.

Container
Large plastic window box: 85cm (34″) long, 20cm (8″) wide, 17½cm (7″) deep.

Plant
Early September to October.

In flower
Mid to end April.

Ingredients
18 dainty yellow multiheaded daffodils *Narcissus triandrus* 'Hawera'.
36 Muscari or grape hyacinths *Muscari armeniacum* 'Heavenly Blue'.
25 litres John Innes No 2 soil.
Drainage material such as small pieces of polystyrene or horticultural grit.

Method
1. Cover the base of the container with 2½cm (1″) drainage material and add 5cm (2″) soil.
2. Plant daffodil bulbs in two rows at the front and back of the box and cover with soil until just their tips show.
3. Now plant the grape hyacinths in between the daffodil bulbs so that their leaves will be less untidy at the front.
4. Cover the bulbs with soil, bringing the level to within 2½cm (1″) of the rim.
5. Water well. Add more soil as necessary to regain its former level.

Aftercare
Maintain soil moisture throughout the Autumn, Winter and particularly in the Spring, but never water in frosty conditions.

After the bulbs have finished flowering they may be planted out in the garden; make sure, however, that they do not dry out until the leaves die down naturally in June or July. Both types of bulbs will do best in a sunny position.

73 TAILOR MADE

Spring weather does not always allow us as much time outside as we may wish for and you may like to consider your window box an extension of the room from which you see it. Here we have a framework of pretty curtains complemented by dainty white arabis and bold red tulips.

Site
Window ledge, some sun.

Container
Large plastic window box 85cm (34″) long, 20cm (8″) wide, 17½cm (7″) deep.

Plant
Early October to mid November.

In flower
The arabis begins to flower in early March and continues for many weeks. The tulips bloom in early April and are excellent for their sturdiness and length of flowering.

Ingredients
18 red double early tulips *Tulipa* 'Stockholm'. For an alternative scheme you could buy pink, yellow, orange or carmine varieties.
 3 pots or 1 strip of white arabis *Arabis caucasica* 'Snowflake'. This begins in Spring as a low growing plant, then with the warmer weather it starts to flower and grows taller. Grown here on a kitchen window sill, it has even reached the height of the tulips.
25 litres John Innes No 2 soil.
Drainage material such as small pieces of polystyrene.

Method
1. Cover the base of the container with 2½cm (1″) drainage material and add 5cm (2″) soil.
2. Plant the tulip bulbs in two rows along the length of the box.

3. Cover the bulbs with soil.
4. If you are using a strip of young plants, remove them from their polystyrene surround and carefully separate them. Whether you are using a strip or pots, space them between the two rows of bulbs so that they will eventually cover the entire box.
5. Make sure all the plants are firmly in place, filling any remaining gaps with soil.
6. Water well. Add more soil if necessary to bring the level to within 2½cm (1″) of the rim.

Aftercare
Maintain soil moisture throughout the Autumn, Winter and particularly in the Spring, but never water in frosty conditions.

After the bulbs have finished flowering they may be planted out in the garden – make sure, however, that they do not dry out until the leaves die down naturally in June or July.

The arabis should be severely cut back, and then planted out in the garden; it likes well drained soil in partial shade. You should be able to use it again for a container display in the Autumn by which time you may wish to divide it.

74 CHILD'S PLAY

This display appears bright and cheery even on a dull Spring day. The vibrant reds and yellows will appeal to any young robot fan, and the planting is so simple even a child could do it.

Site
Window ledge; some sun.

Container
Medium window box: 55cm (22″) long, 15 cm (6″) wide, 12½cm (5″) deep. This one is plastic and has been used to line a wooden box. It means that more than one liner can be planted and used to replace earlier displays as they fade.

Plant
Early October to mid November.

In flower
The tulips should flower in early April with the violas continuing on into Summer.

Ingredients
12 multiheaded red tulips *Tulipa praestans* 'Tubergen's Variety'.
 1 strip of yellow violas or little pansies *Viola cornuta* 'Prince John'.
10 litres John Innes No 2 soil.
Drainage material such as grit or small pieces of polystyrene.

Method
1. Cover the base of the container with 2½cm (1″) drainage material and add 5cm (2″) soil.
2. Plant the tulip bulbs in two rows along the length of the box.

3. Cover with soil.
4. If you are lucky enough to find the violas in the Autumn plant them along the front and back of the box. Firm down well, filling any remaining gaps with soil to bring the level to within 2½cm (1″) of the rim.
5. If you are unable to buy the violas, top up with soil to within 2½cm (1″) of the rim as usual. Then wait until early Spring when you can plant the violas along the front and back of the box between the emerging tulips.
6. Water well. Add more soil if necessary to bring the level to within 2½cm (1″) of the rim.

Aftercare
Maintain soil moisture throughout the Autumn, Winter and particularly in the Spring, but never water in frosty conditions.

After the bulbs have finished flowering they may be planted out in a sunny part of the garden – make sure, however, that they do not dry out until the leaves die down naturally in June or July.

The violas should continue flowering for the rest of the Summer so the plants may be used elsewhere for another display. Remove the flowers to encourage further blooms and feed with a liquid fertiliser as prescribed on the packet or the bottle.

75 PINK AND BLUE

Despite the rain (when this photograph was taken) this still makes a delightful picture. The colours of the curtains are echoed by the soft pink tulips and the carpet of glorious blue muscari hyacinths.

Site
Window ledge, some sun.

Container
Large wooden window box, painted white: 80cm (32″) long, 20cm (8″) wide, 17½cm (7″) deep.

Plant
Early October to mid November.

In flower
Early to late April.

Ingredients
20 pink double early tulips *Tulipa* 'Peach Blossom'.
30 muscari or grape hyacinths *Muscari armeniacum* 'Heavenly Blue'.
25 litres John Innes No 2 soil.
Drainage material such as small pieces of polystyrene.

Method
1. Cover the base of the container with 2½cm (1″) drainage material and add 5cm (2″) soil.
2. Plant the tulip bulbs in two rows along the length of the box.
3. Cover the bulbs with soil until just the tips show.
4. Plant the grape hyacinth bulbs in between the tulips and along the front and back of the box.
5. Cover them with soil.
6. Water well. Add more soil if necessary to bring the level to within 2½cm (1″) of the rim.

Aftercare
Maintain soil moisture throughout the Autumn, Winter and particularly in the Spring, but never water in frosty conditions.

After the bulbs have finished flowering, lift the entire contents of the box and carefully plant them out in a sunny part of the garden. Make sure, however, that they do not dry out until the leaves die down naturally in June or July.

The tulips may bloom spasmodically next season but the grape hyacinths will multiply and flower for years.

76 A BASKET OF EARLY SPRING FLOWERS

What an unusual present to give to a friend or relative. All you need is a deep basket with a high handle and a generous planting of bulbs. Towards the end of March it will be brimming over with rich purple and gold.

Site
Preferably some sun to open up the crocus flowers.

Container
A wicker or bamboo basket: about 50cm (20″) long, 15cm (6″) deep, 40cm (16″) wide with a handle approximately 25–30cm (10–12″) high. It must be given three good coats of yacht varnish to preserve it out of doors.

Plant
Early September to mid October.

In flower
The crocuses will begin to flower in the middle of March and by the end of the month the basket should be in full bloom.

Ingredients
20 early dwarf yellow daffodils *Narcissus cyclamineus* 'February Gold'.
30 purple crocuses *Crocus vernus* 'Purpureus Grandiflorus'.
Moss may be necessary if you have an open bamboo basket as shown above. Use about half a basketful of sphagnum moss or ordinary wreath moss from a florist.
12 litres John Innes No 2 soil.
 2 handfuls of grit.
Plastic sheeting cut to fit the bottom and sides of the basket. Black is best as it won't show against the soil.

Method
1. If you have an open bamboo basket, line it with a generous thickness of moss. Start at the base and bring it well up the sides to form a collar above the rim of the basket.
2. Whatever sort of basket you are using cut six 2½cm (1″) slits in the plastic sheeting and line the base and sides with it.
3. Cover the lining with the grit and add 5cm (2″) soil.
4. Plant the daffodil bulbs first. Divide them equally between the two sides of the basket, then distribute them evenly over the central area. Avoid the part nearest the rim.
5. Cover the daffodil bulbs with soil until just the tips show.
6. Now take half the crocus corms and plant them between the daffodil bulbs. Use the other half to plant around the edge of the basket so as to form a frill.
7. Firm the bulbs and corms into the soil, water lightly and then top up with more soil to bring the level to within 2½cm (1″) of the rim.
8. Any odd pieces of plastic lining which still show should now be trimmed off or tucked under the soil.
9. Find a sheltered home for the basket during the winter, near the wall of the house. It needs moisture so don't cover it.
10. Place it off the ground on four upturned plant pots for the Winter and then when it comes into flower bring it to a prime sunny position near a window so that it can be enjoyed to the full.

Aftercare
•Check that the soil remains moist throughout the Autumn, Winter and particularly in the Spring, but never water in frosty conditions.

After the bulbs have finished flowering, lift them carefully out of the basket and plant direct in the garden. Make sure that they do not dry out until the leaves die down naturally in June or July.

The basket should still be in a good enough state to use again, but take care to give it another three coats of yacht varnish.

77 A BLOOMING BASKET OF TULIPS AND SCILLAS

First the dainty scillas and then the bright red tulips – what a mass of colour to flow out of this simple wicker basket.

Site
A sunny aspect is best.

Container
This is an old wicker basket: 15cm (6″) deep, 25cm (10″) wide, 30cm (12″) long. Almost any wicker basket will do, as long as it is given three good coats of yacht varnish to preserve it out of doors.

Plant
Early October to mid November.

In flower
End March to mid April.

Ingredients
24 multiheaded red tulips *Tulipa praestans* 'Tubergen's Variety'.
20 blue scillas or squills *Scilla sibirica* 'Spring Beauty'.
 6 litres John Innes No 2 soil.
 2 handfuls of grit.
Black plastic sheeting to line the basket.

Method
1. Cut some black plastic sheeting to fit inside the basket and make six 2½cm (1″) slits along the bottom area to provide drainage holes.
2. Cover the liner with the grit and add 2½cm (1″) soil.
3. Gently firm the tulip bulbs into the soil, avoiding contact with each other or with the sides of the basket.
4. Cover the bulbs with soil until just the tips show.
5. Plant some of the scillas between the tulips but concentrate them mainly around the outer edge.
6. Cover with soil and bring the soil level to within 2½cm (1″) of the rim.
7. Water lightly and then top up with more soil if necessary.
8. Any odd pieces of plastic lining which still show should be trimmed off or tucked under the soil.
9. Find a sheltered outdoor home for the basket during the Winter, eg near the wall of the house. It needs moisture so don't cover it.
10. Place the basket off the ground on four upturned plant pots for the Autumn and Winter and then, when it comes into flower, either give it away as a delightful present or bring it into a good sunny spot near a window so that you can enjoy it to the full.

Aftercare
Maintain soil moisture throughout the Autumn, Winter and particularly in the Spring, but never water in frosty conditions.

After the bulbs have finished flowering they may be planted out in the garden. Make sure, however, that they do not dry out until the leaves die down naturally in June or July. The scillas will flower for years; the tulips may not perform as well.

The basket may be used again for a Summer planting but give it another three coats of yacht varnish.

78 A BASKET OF LATE SPRING FLOWERS

Another idea for a basket, this time filled with late Spring flowers. Its initial impact is probably not as great as the previous two, but the pale yellows, pinks and blues make a charming display which will last for weeks.

Site
Partial shade.

Container
Wicker basket: 35cm (14″) long, 22½cm (9″) wide, 20cm (8″) deep. This one has a good high handle, but almost any basket would do. Once filled, don't pick it up by the handle.

Plant
Early September to early October.

In flower
Mid to late April.

Ingredients
30 multiheaded, long lasting dwarf yellow daffodils *Narcissus triandrus* 'Hawera'. (The display would still be lovely with only 20 bulbs).
2 strips or 1 mixed strip pink and blue forget-me-nots *Myosotis alpestris*. If you find it difficult to buy pink or mixed, don't worry – the basket will still look lovely with just blue.
8 litres John Innes No 2 soil.
2 handfuls of grit.
Black plastic bag to line the basket.

Method
1. Cut some black plastic sheeting from the bag to line the basket and make six 2½cm (1″) slits along the bottom to provide drainage holes.
2. Cover the liner with grit and add 5cm (2″) soil.
3. Gently firm the daffodil bulbs into the soil, trying to avoid contact with each other or with the sides of the basket.
4. Cover the bulbs with soil to bring the level to within 2½cm (1″) of the rim.
5. Remove the polystyrene surround to the strips of forget-me-nots and carefully separate the plants. You will only need five of each colour inter-mixed around the edge of the basket. If you were able to buy mixed, use the entire strip.
6. Make sure all the plants are firmly in place.
7. Water well. Add more soil if necessary to bring the level to within 2½cm (1″) of the rim.
8. Any odd pieces of plastic lining still showing should now be trimmed off or tucked into the soil.
9. Find a sheltered outdoor home for the basket during the Winter, eg near the wall of the house. It needs moisture so don't cover it.
10. Raise the basket off the ground on four upturned plant pots for the Autumn and Winter, and then when it comes into flower bring it within view of a window where it can be fully appreciated.

Aftercare
Forget-me-nots like moisture so take care to check that the soil is moist throughout the Autumn, Winter and particularly in the Spring, but never water in frosty conditions.

After the bulbs have finished flowering they may be planted out in the garden. Make sure, however, that they do not dry out until the leaves die down naturally in June or July. The forget-me-nots should be discarded unless you want them to self-seed, in which case, plant them out in the garden. But be warned – they may prove unwelcome guests in years to come!

MISCELLANEOUS SPRING POTS, BARRELS AND A HANGING BASKET

79 TULIPS AND ARABIS

Here we have a tulip with a beautiful flower and very attractive markings on its leaves. The white arabis peeps through and sets off the display well.

Site
Sunny aspect.

Container
Medium sized terracotta 'Cherub' pot: 30cm (12″) in diameter, 25cm (10″) deep.

Plant
November.

In flower
The arabis will begin to flower in March and the tulips in mid April.

Ingredients
13 mid season red tulips *Tulipa kaufmanniana* 'Alfred Cortot'.
 3 pots or one strip of white arabis *Arabis caucasica* 'Snowflake'.
15 litres John Innes No 2 soil.
Crocks or small pieces of polystyrene as drainage material.

Method
1. Cover the base of the container with 2½cm (1″) drainage material and add 5cm (2″) soil.
2. Arrange the tulip bulbs evenly so as to avoid them touching each other or the sides of the pot.
3. Cover the bulbs well with soil.
4. Plant the arabis so that the top of the plants are just below the rim of the pot.
5. Make sure that the plants are firmly in place, filling any remaining gaps with soil.
6. Water well.

Aftercare
Maintain soil moisture throughout the Autumn, Winter and particularly in the Spring, but never water in frosty conditions.

After the bulbs have finished flowering carefully lift the contents of the pot and plant them together in the garden. The arabis should be severely cut back at this time to encourage a well shaped plant for the next season.

80 AN APRIL HANGING BASKET

Here's an idea for a Spring hanging basket, using a few Spring rockery plants, a couple of trailing ivies, and various Spring bulbs. The effect of the pinks and yellows is very pretty.

Site
A sunny sheltered position. Let the basket hang at eye level where all the flowers can be appreciated.

Container
Wire hanging basket: 35cm (14″) diameter with a strong 27½cm (11″) bracket.

Plant
October to mid November.

In flower
Early to late April.

Ingredients
2 *Hedera helix* 'Goldchild'.
8 double early pink tulips *Tulipa* 'Peach Blossom'.
8 multiheaded white daffodils *Narcissus triandrus* 'Thalia'.
6 multiheaded yellow daffodils *Narcissus jonquilla* 'Trevithian'.
3 mid season aubrieta *Aubrieta deltoidea* 'Pink Cascade'.
1 golden alyssum *Alyssum saxatile* 'Flore Pleno'.
10 litres John Innes No 2 soil.
Grit to use as drainage material.
A basketful of moss; spagnum preferably or ordinary wreath moss from a florist's shop.
A plastic circle the size of a dinner plate cut from a plastic bag.

Method
1. Line the basket with a generous thickness of moss, starting at the base and bringing it well up the sides so that you form a collar above the rim of the basket.
2. Cut four 2½cm (1″) slits in the plastic circle and place this over the moss lining in the bottom of the basket.
3. Cover the plastic circle with 5cm (2″) soil.
4. Prise open the wires at the front of the basket, about half way down the side, and plant the alyssum so that it grows outwards through the moss. Its roots should be resting on soil. Take care to close up the wires again and make sure the moss sits snugly all around the plant.

5. Place the two ivies either side of the basket so that they trail over the rim.
6. Plant the three aubrietas between the ivies so that they will spread over the front rim, but avoid the area immediately above the alyssum.
7. Now plant all the bulbs in a mixed group towards the centre of the basket.
8. Cover the bulbs with soil and bring the level up to within 2½cm (1″) of the rim.
9. Make sure the container looks well balanced and that all the plants are firmly in place, filling any remaining gaps with soil.
10. Water well. Add more soil if necessary to bring the level to within 2½cm (1″) of the rim.

Aftercare
Find this basket a sheltered home for the Winter months, but don't cover it up as it needs moisture throughout the Autumn and Winter. In Spring, when all the growth is being made, it will need quite a lot of moisture, so keep a regular check on it. However, never water in frosty conditions.

After the bulbs have finished flowering they may be planted out. Make sure that they do not dry out until the leaves die down naturally in June or July.

The rest of the plants may be used for a display in the Autumn. Plant in a sunny spot and cut them back to ensure a good shape for the next season.

81 A SPRING STRAWBERRY POT

Bulbs often look odd sprouting out of strawberry pots, so here is an idea where the bulbs are only at the top surrounded by pretty little violas around the sides.

Site
Any aspect.

Container
Large terracotta strawberry pot: 42½cm (17″) in diameter, 42½cm (17″) deep.

Plant
Early September to October.

In flower
Early to late April.

Ingredients
20 dwarf yellow daffodils *Narcissus* 'Pencrebar'.
 2 strips of viola of which 1 *Viola tricolor* 'Johnny Jump-Up' yellow and blue, 1 *Viola cornuta* 'Prince John' yellow.
60 litres John Innes No 2 soil.
Plenty of gravel as drainage material.

Method
1. Cover the base of the container with 2½cm (1″) drainage material.
2. To help drainage further, take a long cardboard tube and place it on its end in the middle of the pot. Fill it with gravel, and surround it with soil.
3. As the soil level gets higher, firm it down, and plant the viola through the holes in the side of the pot. (You may be unable to buy the viola at this time of year, in which case just fill the pot with soil until you reach the top third).
4. Plant the daffodil bulbs evenly around the tube.
5. Bring the soil level to within 2½cm (1″) of the rim of the pot.
6. Carefully remove the cardboard tube.
7. Plant the remaining violas in the top of the pot, putting 'Prince John' in the centre and 'Johnny Jump-Up' around the edge.

8. Water very carefully to minimize loss of soil through the holes. In time this will not pose a problem as the viola roots will secure the soil.

Aftercare
Maintain soil moisture throughout the Autumn, Winter and particularly in the Spring, but never water in frosty conditions.

If you have been unable to obtain the violas in the Autumn buy them in early Spring and put one or more in each hole, leaving the rest for the top. Save some yellow ones for the centre. When the bulbs have finished flowering they may be planted out in the garden. Make sure, however, that they do not dry out until the leaves die down naturally in June or July.

The violas may also be planted out so that you can enjoy their flowers for the rest of the Summer. Deadheading and a regular liquid feed will prolong the flowering period.

82 BULBS IN A WALLPOT

This is a very small wall-pot and the planting area is limited, therefore it is best to choose mul-tiheaded bulbs. Here we have a succession. Red tulips to begin with, fol-lowed by *Tulipa tarda*. In this way, just a handful of bulbs can give a colour-ful, but extended show.

Site
A sunny wall position.

Container
Small terracotta wallpot: 30cm (12″) in diameter, 20cm (8″) deep.

Plant
Mid October to mid November.

In flower
Early to late April.

Ingredients
4 multiheaded early tulips *Tulipa praestans* 'Tubergen's Variety'.
8 multiheaded late tulips *Tulipa tarda*; these tend to flop rather than remain upright.
5 litres John Innes No 2 soil.
Gravel or small pieces of polystyrene as drainage material.

Method
1. Cover the base of the container with 2½cm (1″) drainage material and 5cm (2″) soil.

2. These bulbs are very small and should be arranged in two layers. Plant the 'Tubergen's Variety' at the bottom, and cover with soil so that just the tips show. Then plant the *Tulipa tarda* in between.
3. Cover wtih more soil, bringing the level to within 2½cm (1″) of the rim.
4. Water well. Add more soil if necessary to regain the former level.

Aftercare
Maintain soil moisture throughout the Autumn, Winter and particularly in the Spring, but never water in frosty conditions.

After the bulbs have finished flowering they may be planted out in a sunny place in the garden. Make sure, however, that they do not dry out until the leaves die down naturally in June or July. It is unlikely that they will do very well next season and you may prefer to throw them away.

83 A BARREL OF WALLFLOWERS AND TULIPS

The pale primrose wallflowers, and violet tulips make an appealing colour scheme. A gentle fragrance comes from the wallflowers, filling the late Spring air.

Site
Prefers a sunny spot, sheltered from strong winds.

Container
A wooden tub or half barrel: a 60cm (24″) in diameter, 42½cm (17″) deep.

Plant
Early October.

In flower
From mid April to end May.

Ingredients
1 bunch or strip of dwarf wallflowers *Cheiranthus* 'Primrose Bedder'.
10 late medium tall tulips *Tulipa* 'Atilla' of the Triumph type.
100 litres John Innes No 2 soil.
Plenty of crocks or pieces of polystyrene as drainage material.

Method
1. If you buy a bunch (rather than a strip) of wallflower plants, separate them as soon as possible, discarding any very weak ones. Give the rest a good drink until they have visibly revived.
2. Cover the base of the container with 5cm (2″) drainage material and cover with 20cm (8″) soil.
3. Plant six of the tulip bulbs in a wide circle leaving four for the centre.
4. Cover the bulbs with soil until just the tips show.
5. Choose eight of the best developed wallflowers, make a circle of five of them near the outer edge, and three in the centre but avoid placing directly over the tulips. Add soil around each one until the base of the stem is covered. If you have a garden you may like to plant out the remaining plants, then if you lose any of the ones in the pot (and you may), you will have a replacement.
6. Water well. Firm down the plants and top up with soil where necessary, leaving at least a 2½cm (1″) gap between the soil and the rim of the barrel.

Aftercare
Maintain soil moisture throughout the Autumn, Winter and Spring but never water in frosty weather.

Wind seems to do more damage than heavy snow or frost, so try to place the pot in a sheltered area. When the wallflowers have finished flowering discard them. Lift the tulips with as many of the roots intact as possible and replant them in a sunny spot in the garden.

84 TRADITION WITH A DIFFERENCE

Wallflowers and tulips are a traditional combination. Usually the tulips tower above the wallflowers. These tulips, however, are slightly shorter but no less bold. Their brilliant colour and their fullness of flower creates an exciting picture with the purple wallflowers.

Site
A sunny spot, sheltered from strong winds.

Container
A wooden tub or half barrel: 60cm (24″) in diameter, 42½cm (17″) deep.

Plant
Early October.

In flower
From Mid April to end May.

Ingredients
1 bunch or strip of wallflowers *Cheiranthus* 'Rose Queen' 45cm (18″) high.
20 double late tulips *Tulipa* 'Bonanza'.
100 litres John Innes No 2 soil.
Plenty of large crocks or pieces of polystyrene for drainage material.

Method
1. If you bought a bunch (rather than a strip) of wallflowers, separate them as soon as possible. Any very weak ones may be discarded. Then give the rest a good drink until they have visibly revived.
2. Cover the base of the container with 5cm (2″) of drainage material and add 20cm (8″) soil.
3. Plant 14 tulip bulbs in a circle near the edge of the barrel, and the rest in an inner circle.
4. Cover the bulbs with soil until just the tips show.
5. Choose eight of the best developed plants, make a circle of five of them near the outer edge, and place three in the centre but avoid placing them directly over the tulips. Add soil around each one until the base of the stem is covered. If you have a garden you may like to plant out the remaining plants, then if you lose any of the ones in the container (and you may), you will have a replacement.

6. Water well. Firm down the plants and top up with soil where necessary, leaving at least a 2½cm (1″) gap between the soil and the rim of the barrel.

Aftercare
Maintain the soil moisture throughout the Autumn, Winter and Spring but never water in frosty weather.

Wind seems to do more damage to the wallflowers than heavy snow or frost, so try to place the barrel in a sheltered area. Discard the wallflowers when they have finished flowering.

Lift the tulips with as many of their roots intact as possible and replant them in a sunny spot in the garden. Make sure that they do not dry out until the leaves die down naturally in June or July. They may flower only spasmodically next season.

85 FORGET-ME-NOTS AND DAFFODILS

These creamy whites, pinks and blues make a simple, dainty picture.

Site
Any aspect.

Container
A medium sized pot:
35cm (14″) in diameter,
30cm (12″) deep.

Plant
Early September to October.

In flower
Mid April to May.

Ingredients
12 multiheaded, late flowering daffodils *Narcissus* 'Sir Winston Churchill'.
2 strips or 1 mixed strip of pink and blue forget-me-not *Myosotis alpestris*.
25 litres John Innes No 2 soil.
Crocks or small pieces of polystyrene as drainage material.

Method
1. Cover the base of the container with 2½cm (1″) drainage material and add 10cm (4″) soil.
2. Arrange the daffodil bulbs evenly over the soil, firm in, and cover with more soil, bringing the level to within 2½cm (1″) of the rim.
3. Carefully separate the forget-me-not plants. You will only need four of each colour intermixed around the edge of the pot; if you were able to buy mixed plants use the entire strip.
4. Make sure the forget-me-nots are firmly planted.
5. Water well.

Aftercare
Forget-me-nots like plenty of water, so take care to check soil moisture throughout the Autumn, Winter and particularly in the Spring, but never water in frosty conditions.

After the bulbs have finished flowering they may be planted out in the garden. The forget-me-nots should be discarded unless you want them to self seed, in which case plant them out in the garden. Be warned, however, they may be unwelcome guests in years to come.

86 DAFFODILS AND TULIPS

'White Lion' is one of the most beautiful double headed daffodils. Here it is mixed with a brilliant red tulip to make an outstanding show. Why do some people say that daffodils and tulips should never be mixed?

Site
Sunny if possible.

Container
A medium terracotta 'Florentine Square' pot: 30cm (12″) in depth, width and height.

Plant
October to early November.

In flower
Mid April.

Ingredients
10 double mid season daffodils *Narcissus* 'White Lion'.
12 mid season short red tulips *Tulipa greigii* 'Oriental Beauty'.
26 litres John Innes No 2 soil.
Crocks or small pieces of polystyrene as drainage material.

Method
1. Cover the base of the container with 2½cm (1″) drainage material and add 10cm (4″) soil.
2. Plant the tulip bulbs around the edge of the pot and the daffodil bulbs in the centre. Avoid them touching either each other or the sides of the container.
3. Bring soil level to within 2½cm (1″) of the rim.
4. Water well and add more soil as necessary to regain the former level.

Aftercare
Maintain the soil moisture throughout the Autumn, Winter and particularly in the Spring, but never water in frosty conditions.

After the bulbs have finished flowering, lift them carefully out of the pot and plant them together in a sunny part of the garden. Make sure that they do not lack water until the leaves die down naturally in June or July.

The tulips may not flower well next season but the daffodils should give years of pleasure.

87 A WEDDING DAY POT

This charming combination makes a perfect display to grace any Spring wedding, although you don't have to have an excuse to plant it!

Site
Some sun preferred.

Container
Large terracotta pot: 37½cm (15″) in diameter, 37½cm (15″) deep.

Plant
Early October to early November.

In flower
This kind of arabis will flower in early April followed by the bulbs in the middle of the month.

Ingredients
 7 white mid season tulips *Tulipa* 'White Virgin'.
 8 pink trumpet daffodils *Narcissus* 'Salome'; the trumpets will begin as yellow and then change to apricot pink as they mature.
 3 large double white arabis *Arabis caucasica* 'Flore Pleno'.
43 litres John Innes No 2 soil.
Crocks or pieces of polystyrene as drainage material.

Method
1. Cover the base of the container with 2½cm (1″) drainage material and add 15cm (6″) soil.
2. Arrange five daffodil bulbs in a circle about 10cm (4″) from the edge of the pot, with three more in the middle.
3. Cover the bulbs with the soil until just the tips show, then plant the tulip bulbs in a slightly smaller circle than the daffodils.

4. Bring the soil level to within 2½cm (1″) of the rim.
5. Plant the arabis around the edge of the container, making sure that they are firmly in place.
6. Water well. Add more soil if necessary to bring the level to within 2½cm (1″) of the rim.

Aftercare
Maintain soil moisture throughout the Autumn, Winter and particularly in the Spring, but never water in frosty conditions.

After the bulbs have finished flowering they may be planted out in the garden. Make sure, however, that they do not dry out until the leaves die down naturally in June or July.

Tulips prefer a sunny home but be warned – these might not perform well in future seasons. Arabis likes partial shade. Now is the time to cut it back to encourage a good shape for next season.

88 AN IDEA FOR A CHIMNEY POT

Sunshine really brings out the best in this striking combination of crocuses and tulips. Cascades of variegated ivy cover the front of the chimney pot, setting off the whole picture.

Site
Best in a sunny aspect.

Container
A small plastic or terracotta container to fit inside the top of the chimney pot. Choose as large a one as possible but make sure it doesn't sit too proud in the chimney pot. This one has a 22½cm (9″) diameter and is 22½cm (9″) tall. It was slightly on the small side so we just wedged it with a piece of wood. The actual chimney pot can be any size although the really big ones can be quite heavy to move.

Plant
Early October to mid November.

In flower
Middle to end of March.

Ingredients
12 Dutch white crocuses *Crocus vernus* 'Jeanne D'Arc'.
12 early dwarf tulips *Tulipa kaufmanniana* 'Shakespeare'.
 2 variegated ivies *Hedera helix* 'Heise'.
10 litres John Innes No 2 soil.
Drainage material such as crocks or small pieces of polystyrene.

Method
1. Cover the base of the inner container with 2½cm (1″) drainage material and add 5cm (2″) soil.
2. Place both ivies at the front.
3. Plant the tulip bulbs in a group behind the ivies.
4. Cover with soil until just the tips of the bulbs remain.
5. Plant the crocus corms in between the tulips and save a few for the gap between the two ivies.
6. Firm down the ivies and top up with soil to within 2½cm (1″) of the rim.

7. Water well. Add more soil if necessary to return the level to within 2½cm (1″) of the rim.
8. Lift the pot and place it carefully in the chimney pot, wedging it if necessary with a piece of wood.

Aftercare
Maintain soil moisture throughout the Autumn, Winter and particularly in the Spring, but never water in frosty conditions.

After the bulbs have finished flowering, the entire contents of the pot may be carefully lifted, the ivies separated, and the bulbs planted out together in a sunny spot in the garden. However, make sure that they do not dry out until the leaves die down naturally in June or July.

The ivies may be used for another display in the Autumn. They are not fussy and can be planted anywhere in the garden.

89 MIXED TULIPS

Another idea for mixed tulips. An easy planting which will brighten even a dull Spring day.

Site
Sunny if possible.

Container
White plastic tub: 32½cm (13″) in diameter, 32½cm (13″) deep.

Plant
Mid October to mid November.

In flower
Mid April.

Ingredients
10 mid season white tulips *Tulipa* 'White Virgin'.
10 mid season pinky-red tulips *Tulipa undulatifolia* (syn. *T. eichleri*).
23 litres John Innes No 2 soil.
Crocks or small pieces of polystyrene as drainage material.

Method
1. Cover the base of the container with 2½cm (1″) drainage material and add 15cm (6″) soil.
2. Alternate the bulbs planting them evenly over the surface, but avoid them touching either each other or the sides of the pot.
3. Cover with soil so that the level reaches within 2½cm (1″) of the rim.
4. Water well. Add more soil if necessary to regain the former level.

Aftercare
Maintain soil moisture throughout the Autumn, Winter and particularly in the Spring, but never water in frosty conditions.

After the bulbs have finished flowering, lift them very carefully and plant them together in a sunny part of the garden. Make sure that they do not dry out until the leaves die down naturally in June or July. Be warned, however, they may not flower well next season.

90 TULIPS AND FORGET-ME-NOTS

Red Riding Hood is a well known tulip with strong markings on its leaves. Here, it is underplanted with forget-me-nots.

Site
Sunny aspect.

Container
Medium sized terracotta 'Cherub' pot: 30cm (12″) in diameter, 25cm (10″) deep.

Plant
November.

In flower
Late April.

Ingredients
14 short red tulips *Tulipa greigii* 'Red Riding Hood'.
 1 strip or 4 plants of blue forget-me-not *Myosotis alpestris*.
15 litres John Innes No 2 soil.
Crocks or small pieces of polystyrene as drainage material.

Method
1. Cover the base of the container with 2½cm (1″) drainage material and add 5cm (2″) soil.
2. Arrange the tulip bulbs evenly so as to avoid them touching either each other or the sides of the container.
3. Cover them with soil bringing the level up to within 2½cm (1″) of the rim.
4. Plant forget-me-nots around the edge of the container. If you are using a strip of plants carefully separate them before planting.
5. Make sure the plants are firmly in place. Water well. Add more soil if necessary to bring level to within 2½cm (1″) of the rim.

Aftercare
Maintain soil moisture throughout Autumn, Winter and particularly in the Spring, but never water in frosty conditions.

After the bulbs have finished flowering they may be planted out in a sunny part of the garden. Make sure, however, that they do not dry out until the leaves die down naturally in June or July.

The forget-me-nots should be discarded unless you want them to self seed, in which case plant them in the garden. But be warned, they can be very prolific.

91 TULIPS GALORE

These tulips create a magnificent picture of bold yellow and white, surrounded by pale blue forget-me-nots. When you walk past them, you can't help but notice the wonderful dark centres of the yellow ones. Hence the angle of this photograph.

Site
Sunny aspect.

Container
Large terracotta pot: 55cm (22″) in diameter, 42½cm (17″) deep.

Plant
Mid October to mid November.

In flower
Mid to late April on into May.

Ingredients
  18 white mid season tulips *Tulipa* 'White Virgin'.
  19 yellow mid season tulips *Tulipa* 'Beauty of Apeldoorn', yellow with an orange flush.
   1 strip or 4 plants of blue forget-me-nots *Myosotis alpestris*.
100 litres John Innes No 2 soil.
Pieces of polystyrene or large crocks as drainage material.

Method
1. Cover the base of the container with 5cm (2″) drainage material and 15cm (6″) soil.
2. Plant the 'Beauty of Apeldoorn' bulbs first, distributing them evenly.
3. Cover them with soil until just their tips show and then plant the 'White Virgin' in between.
4. Bring the soil level up to within 2½cm (1″) of the rim.
5. If using a strip, carefully separate the forget-me-nots and plant them around the edge of the container. Make sure they are firmed in. Water well.

Aftercare
Forget-me-nots like plenty of water, so take care to check the soil moisture throughout the Autumn, Winter and particularly in the Spring, but never water in frosty conditions. We noticed the 'Beauty of Apeldoorn' in the garden were much taller and larger flowered than the ones in this pot. The close planting in the pot must have restricted their growth which, in this instance, was a good thing.

After the tulips have finished flowering they may be planted out in a sunny part of the garden. Make sure, however, that they do not dry out until the leaves die down naturally in June or July. The more care you take to minimize root disturbance, the better the chance of good flowers next year.

The forget-me-nots should be discarded unless you want them to self seed, in which case plant them out in the garden. But be warned, they may be unwelcome guests in years to come.

92 A CHOICE FOR THE FRONT DOOR

The white tulips and blue grape hyacinths make a simple but effective combination.

Site
Sunny position if possible.

Container
Tall terracotta 'Cherub' pot: 30cm (12″) in diameter, 35cm (14″) deep.

Plant
November.

In flower
Mid to late April.

Ingredients
6 white mid season tulips *Tulipa* 'White Virgin'.
24 muscari or grape hyacinth *Muscari armeniacum* 'Heavenly Blue'.
20 litres John Innes No 2 soil.
Small pieces of polystyrene as drainage material.

Method
1. Cover the base of the container with 5cm (2″) drainage material and add 10cm (4″) soil.
2. Plant the six tulip bulbs in a wide circle and cover with soil until just their tips show.
3. Plant the grape hyacinth bulbs in two circles so that they will grow up either side of the tulips.
4. Cover with soil and bring the level to within 2½cm (1″) of the rim.
5. Water well. Add more soil if necessary to regain the former level.

Aftercare
Maintain soil moisture throughout the Autum, Winter and particularly in the Spring, but never water in frosty conditions.

After the bulbs have finished flowering they may be planted out in a sunny part of the garden. Make sure, however, that they do not dry out until the leaves die down naturally in June or July.

The grape hyacinths should multiply and give a good show for years to come; the tulips may not perform so well.

SPRING RECIPES WITHOUT BULBS

93 A DAINTY WALLPOT

A simple idea using golden alyssum and blue forget-me-nots.

Site
A sunny wall.

Container
A small terracotta wallpot: 10cm (4″) in diameter, 12½cm (5″) deep.

Plant
October.

In flower
Mid April to May.

Ingredients
1 pot of blue forget-me-nots *Myosotis alpestris*.
1 pot of double golden alyssum *Alyssum saxatile* 'Flore Pleno'.
1 litre John Innes No 2 soil.
A good handful of grit.

Method
1. Cover the base of the container with the grit and 2½cm (1″) soil.
2. Plant the alyssum and forget-me-nots side by side.
3. Make sure the plants are firmly in place, filling any remaining gaps with soil.
4. Water well. Add more soil if necessary.

Aftercare
The pot will soon dry out so take care to maintain soil moisture throughout the Autumn, Winter and

particularly in the Spring, but never water in frosty conditions.

The alyssum may be used for another display in the Autumn, and should be severely cut back and then planted out in a sunny spot in the garden. The forget-me-nots should be discarded unless you like them to self seed in which case you can plant them out in the garden as well. But be warned, they may prove a nuisance in the future.

94 BORROWED FROM THE COUNTRY

The blue of the forget-me-nots and the yellow of the cowslips make a pretty combination of Spring flowers. They bring a hint of the country to a town window sill. No need to plant until March, it's simple to care for and delightful to watch as it grows.

Site
Window ledge; sunny aspect.

Container
Medium window box (wooden with a plastic liner): 55cm (22″) long, 15cm (6″) wide, 12½cm (5″) deep.

Plant
March.

In flower
April and May.

Ingredients
3 cowslips *Primula veris* (these have grown larger than the wild ones).
4 pots or 1 strip blue forget-me-nots *Myosotis alpestris*.
10 litres John Innes No 2 soil.
Small pieces of polystyrene as drainage material.

Method
1. Cover the base of the container with 2½cm (1″) drainage material and add 10cm (4″) soil.
2. Space the three cowslips along the middle of the box.
3. Plant the forget-me-nots around the cowslips; if you are using a strip of plants carefully separate before planting.
4. Make sure the plants are firmly in place, filling any remaining gaps with soil.
5. Water well. Add more soil if necessary.

Aftercare
All these plants like moisture so check that the soil never becomes too dry. You will soon see by the wilting leaves.

After the cowslips have finished flowering they may be planted in a sunny spot in the garden.

The forget-me-nots should be discarded unless you like them to self seed in which case you can plant them out in the garden. But be warned, they may prove too prolific in the future.

95 SPRING FLOWERS BUT NO BULBS

This is a dual purpose box. In the Autumn it housed cyclamen and solanums and the alyssum, now in the Spring it is the home of calceolaria and polyanthus.

Site
Window ledge, sunny sheltered aspect.

Container
Large terracotta window box: 80cm (32″) long, 20cm (8″) wide, 17½cm (7″) deep.

Plant
Early September and again in April.

In flower
The cyclamen and solanum will last from the time of planting until the first really sharp frost; the Spring display will last from early April to late May.

Ingredients
3 pink pot-plant cyclamen *Cyclamen persicum* 'Perfection Mixed'; choose ones with erect foliage and plenty of flowerbuds underneath.
2 pot-plant solanums or Winter Cherries *Solanum capsicastrum* 'Covent Garden', height 30cm (12″).
3 Spring rock garden plants *Alyssum saxatile* 'Flore Pleno', double golden yellow.
2 pot-plant calceolarias or slipper plants *Calceolaria* x *herbeohybrida*.
4 tall red polyanthus.
25 litres John Innes No 2 soil.
Small pieces of polystyrene as drainage material.

NB If you only want the Spring display shown in the photograph ignore instructions 3–7.

Method
1. Cover the base of the container with 2½cm (1″) drainage material and add 10cm (4″) soil.
2. Plant the alyssums at the front of the box so that they will trail down the front, one in the centre and one at each end.
3. Plant the two solanums either side of the centre.

4. Plant three empty plant pots to mark the position of the cyclamen.
5. Water well and then raise the soil level to within 2½cm (1″) of the rim.
6. Remove the plant pots and plant the cyclamen.
7. When the solanums and cyclamen are past their best remove them.
8. In early April, when the weather warms up, plant the polyanthus, two together in the centre and one at either end; then plant the calceolaria in between the polyanthus, as shown in the photograph.
9. Water well and top up with soil if necessary to bring the level back to within 2½cm (1″) of the rim.

Aftercare
Maintain soil moisture throughout the Autumn, Winter and the Spring, but never water in frosty conditions.

Avoid direct watering of the cyclamen as their needs are less than the other plants. On the other hand solanums and polyanthus are thirsty drinkers and will soon let you know when they are feeling dry – keep a special watch over them.

When the calceolaria have finished flowering, discard them. Cut back the alyssum and then replant them in a sunny spot in the garden. The polyanthus may be planted out as well.

96 WALLFLOWERS AND BELLIS DAISIES

Here is an idea for underplanting pale yellow wall-flowers with pretty pink bellis. Together they form a fragrant pyramid which will last for many weeks.

Site
Sunny aspect, sheltered from strong winds.

Container
Medium sized terracotta pot; 35cm (14″) in diameter, 30cm (12″) deep.

Plant
Early October. In some areas you may have to wait until early Spring for the bellis.

In flower
From early Spring until the end of May.

Ingredients
1 bunch or 1 strip of dwarf wallflowers *Cheiranthus* 'Primrose Bedder' 30cm (12″) high.
1 strip of pink daisies *Bellis perennis* 'Dresden China'.
28 litres John Innes No 2 soil.
Pieces of polystyrene or crocks as drainage material.

Method
1. If you have a bunch (rather than a strip) of wallflower plants, separate them as soon as possible. Any weak ones may be discarded. Then give the rest a good drink until they have visibly revived.
2. Cover the base of the container with 5cm (2″) drainage material and add about 15cm (6″) soil.
3. Choose seven of the best developed plants and make a circle of five of them near the outer edge. Add soil around each one until the base of the stem is covered. Then plant the remaining two in the central area, again mounding up the soil around the roots until the base of the stem is covered. If you have a garden you may like to plant out the smaller plants, then if you lose any of the ones in the pot (and you may) you will have a replacement.
4. If you are able to buy bellis in the Autumn, carefully separate the plants in the strip and

insert around the edge of the pot. You might have to wait until early Spring, when you will find them more readily available.
5. Water well, firming down the plants, and topping up with soil where necessary. Leave at least 2½cm (1″) between the soil level and the rim of the pot.

Aftercare
Maintain the soil moisture throughout the Autumn, Winter and Spring but never water in frosty conditions.

Wind seems to do more damage to the wallflowers than heavy snow or frost, so try to place the pot in a sheltered area.

When the wallflowers have finished flowering, empty the pot and discard all the contents although the bellis could be enjoyed for several more weeks in the garden if preferred.

INSTANT SPRING COLOUR

97 A SPRING POT WHICH WILL GO ON INTO SUMMER

Sometimes you feel you just can't wait until the end of May to plant out your pots for the Summer. Here is an example of what you can put together to achieve lovely colour from early April onwards even though night frosts may still occur.

Site
Any aspect.

Container
Small terracotta pot: 25cm (10″) in diameter, 20cm (8″) deep.

Plant
Early April onwards.

In flower
From time of planting.

Ingredients
3 pale blue pansies *Viola* x *wittrockiana*.
1 strip of pink daisies *Bellis perennis* 'Dresden China', 7½–15cm (3–6″) high.
8 litres John Innes No 2 soil.
Small crocks or pieces of polystyrene as drainage material.

Method
1. Cover the base of the container with 2½cm (1″) drainage material and add 7½cm (3″) soil.
2. Plant the pansies towards the centre of the pot and fill the gaps with soil.
3. Carefully separate the bellis plants and plant them around the edge.
4. Water well. Add more soil if necessary.

Aftercare
Check the soil moisture regularly and water generously, particularly in warm spells. Pansies especially like a lot of moisture. Feed with a proprietary brand as directed, at least every two weeks. The pansies will flower for longer if deadheaded. Discard them when they have finally given up flowering.

98 AN INSTANT DISPLAY IN A VERSAILLES TUB

If you can't be bothered with bulbs, and you want an early display of flowers, the easiest answer is to buy some colourful polyanthus. Add some height with a conifer and some depth with a couple of trailing ivies and you will immediately have an interesting display to last you all through the Spring.

Site
A terrace, or next to your front door; any aspect.

Container
This is a 37½cm (15") square Versailles tub; but any medium-to-large barrel or pot would suit.

Plant
Early Spring, as soon as the polyanthus are available.

In flower
From time of planting until late May.

Ingredients
6 large polyanthus; either one colour or mixed.
2 variegated ivies *Hedera helix* 'Goldchild'. Choose ones with long trails.
1 box, bay, or, as seen here, golden conifer *Cupressus macrocarpa* 'Goldcrest', this is at least 42½cm (17") tall which adds central height.
40 litres John Innes No 2 soil.
Drainage material such as small pieces of polystyrene.
Plastic sheeting to line the tub.

Method
1. The bottom of the tub has moveable wooden slats. Cover these with the plastic sheeting in which six or more 2½cm (1") slits have been cut.
2. Add 10cm (4") drainage material, then top up with soil leaving about 10cm (4") clear at the top.

3. Plant the ivies in the two front corners of the tub, position the cupressus in the centre, and arrange the polyanthus around it.
4. Make sure the container looks well balanced and that all the plants are firmly in place, filling any remaining gaps with soil.
5. Water well.

Aftercare
The polyanthus like moisture so keep the tub well watered in warm spells.

After the polyanthus have finished flowering, remove from the tub and plant out in the garden along with the rest of the plants. If you choose to use the ivies and cupressus in a Summer display just leave them in place. (See Recipe 135, page 164.)

99 THE SAME THEME BUT MORE EXTRAVAGANT

This is more costly than the previous idea, but it gives a much fuller look to the tub.

Site
A terrace, or next to your front door; any aspect.

Container
This is a 37½cm (15″) square Versailles tub, but any medium to large pot or barrel would suit.

Plant
Early April as soon as the weather begins to warm up.

In flower
From time of planting until end May.

Ingredients
3 large yellow polyanthus.
3 cinerarias *Senecio* x *hybridus* (*Cineraria cruenta*); usually sold as house plants. Look for compact plants with lots of buds. Light blue makes a good contrast with the yellow polyanthus. You may also like to add a different central colour as in this example.
2 variegated ivies *Hedera helix* 'Goldchild'. Choose ones with long trails.
1 golden conifer, at least 42½cm (17″) high, *Cupressus macrocarpa* 'Goldcrest'.
50 litres John Innes No 2 soil.
Small pieces of polystyrene as drainage material.
Plastic sheeting to line the tub.

Method
1. The bottom of the tub has moveable wooden slats. Cover these with the plastic sheeting in which six or more 2½cm (1″) slits have been made.
2. Add 10cm (4″) drainage material, then top up with soil leaving about 10cm (4″) clear at the top.
3. Plant the two ivies at the two front corners of the tub, and position the cupressus at the centre back.
4. Plant the tallest of the three polyanthus right in front of the cupressus and the other two behind the ivies.
5. Plant the blue cinerarias at each back corner, and plant the pink one in the centre front of the tub.
6. Make sure the container looks well balanced and that all the plants are firmly in place, filling any remaining gaps with soil.
7. Water well.

Aftercare
Keep the tub well watered, particularly in warm spells.

After the plants have finished flowering, discard the cinerarias, remove the rest of the plants from the tub and replant in a shady moist spot in the garden. However, if you wish to use the ivies and the cupressus in a Summer display, just leave them in place (see Recipe 135, page 164).

100 AN INSTANT SPRING HANGING BASKET

Here is an instant Spring hanging basket. It looks full and bright, and will continue to flower for many weeks.

Site
Lovely by the front door, but don't put the bracket too high. You want to be able to look into it, not up at it. Any aspect.

Container
Hanging basket: 30cm (12″) in diameter. You will also need a 22½cm (9″) bracket.

Plant
April, as soon as the weather warms up.

In flower
From time of planting until end of May.

Ingredients
3 cinerarias *Senecio* x *hybridus* (*Cineraria cruenta*). These are often sold as houseplants. Look for compact plants with lots of buds. It is useful to have a slightly bigger plant for the central position, which may be a different colour to the two others.
2 yellow primroses *Primula vulgaris.*
2 variegated ivies *Hedera helix* 'Goldchild'. Choose large plants with long trails.
10 litres John Innes No 2 soil or a peat-based compost.
1 basketful of sphagnum moss or ordinary wreath moss from a florists.
Plastic lining cut in the shape of a dinner plate. Any reasonably strong plastic bag will do.

Method
1. Line the basket with a generous thickness of moss: start at the base and bring it well up the sides so that you form a collar above the rim of the basket.
2. Cut four 2½cm (1″) slits in the plastic lining, then put it in place at the bottom of the basket.
3. Cover the base of the lining with 10cm (4″) soil.
4. Position the two ivies to trail over the sides of the basket, where two of the chains meet the rim.
5. Plant the two primroses beside the ivies towards the centre front of the basket.
6. At this stage fill in with soil around the ivies and primroses.
7. Plant the two blue cinerarias, one at the front of

the basket so that it sits snugly between the two yellow primroses with its leaves over the front rim, and the other at the back of the basket between the two ivies.
8. Fill in as necessary with more soil and then place the last cineraria in position right in the crown of the basket.
9. Water well. This will be easier if you use a watering can with a long spout that can get in between the dense foliage of the cineraria.

Aftercare
Water as necessary to maintain moist soil. Feed with a liquid fertiliser every two weeks.

When the cineraria have finished flowering, remove and discard. Replant the primroses and ivies in a shady position in the garden.

The moss and plastic lining may be used again for a Summer planting so leave them intact.

SUMMER RECIPES

INTRODUCTION TO THE SUMMER RECIPES

High Summer is surely the time when everyone wants to make the best use of their containers. Lovely hanging baskets, billowing window boxes and sumptuous pots – we hope you will find something to suit you in the recipes which follow.

The recipes might be especially fragrant, they may create a certain shape or a particular colour scheme which you like. But remember, there is nothing magical about them. We would be the first to agree that in many cases a light blue lobelia will look just as good as a dark blue one. The same applies to many of the different fuchsias, begonias and geraniums. So don't be dismayed if you can't buy exactly the same ones as appear in the recipes. Just try to buy those of a similar nature and the results will probably be equally good.

A few words on our choice of plants. Many of our recipes use the usual Summer container plants such as geraniums, fuchsias, lobelias, etc. These are all readily available in May and should not prove difficult to obtain. But we have also made use of tuberous begonias which give such a brilliant and long lasting display. If you buy them as growing plants in May you will find them quite expensive and the colour range probably a little restricted. The answer to this problem is to buy them in late Winter – early Spring as dry tubers in the garden centres. You will then have a good choice of colours and find out that they are quite reasonable in cost. It will involve you in more work but they are not difficult to get started. The same applies to lilies. You can buy them in bud in May but they are infinitely cheaper to buy as bulbs in February. Moreover, we have used several plants which will be generally unobtainable other than in seed form. Dwarf sweetpeas, dwarf nasturtiums and lime green tobacco plants are some examples. Think ahead and buy them in March or earlier. They are easy to germinate and of course a very cheap way of filling your containers.

WATERING
If there is any one key to the success of these displays, it is in the watering of them. Always be generous and patient and don't expect a hanging basket to absorb a gallon of water in seconds. Pour some on, attend to the deadheading, pour some more, wait again and so on until the container is really wet all over. The same with barrels and boxes. Give them a drink and then wait for it to soak in. Then give them another.

It is often better to apply water at soil level rather than from overhead. The flowers will spoil with heavy overhead watering, particularly petunias. Never water under the midday sun. The leaves would scorch and the plant would suffer. Wait until the evening or do it in the early morning before the sun has a chance to gather strength.

FEEDING
Feeding is also important. Once flowering has begun most plants benefit from liquid feed. If you have used John Innes soil then additional feeding is less necessary; indeed geraniums and Livingstone daisies hardly seem to need it at all. But if you have used a peat-based compost, regular feeding is essential. Always do the usual water before applying a liquid feed so that the container will easily soak up the nutrients.

DEADHEADING
Deadheading is the removal of the flower and potential seed pod in order to conserve the plant's energy for producing more flowers. It is another important task. Regular efforts will bring noticeable results, particularly with sweetpeas, gazanias, fuchsias, roses, marguerites, verbena and Livingstone daisies.

SPRAYING
Spraying against insects is essential too. Blackfly on nasturtiums, or greenfly on petunias can ruin the plants in just a matter of days. But if you spray as soon as you notice them, and then again two or three days later, you should be able to keep the insects in check.

There is nothing new in all this advice. If you follow it, you should obtain some lovely results. Treat your plants with the care and attention they deserve and you will be justly rewarded.

GUIDANCE FOR PRE- AND POST-SEASONAL CARE

BEGONIAS (tuberous)

Autumn Their leaves will start to turn yellow which indicates the start of their dying process. Label them and lift them in early October so as to avoid any frost damage. Plant them temporarily in some moist peat. Gradually reduce their supply of water. When the foliage has died down completely, remove the tubers, clean the soil off and store them in a cool frost-free environment 7–10°C (45–50°F) covered with dry peat until around Christmas. You should then give the occasional light watering to prevent shrivelling of the tubers.

Spring Start the new or your old tubers into growth again in early Spring by planting them in individual pots or spare window boxes filled with a moist peat-based compost.

The tubers should be bedded into the top of the soil, hollow side uppermost, so that they are nestling into it without being entirely covered. Put the pot or window box into your airing cupboard if you have one, or any other warm place until the tubers have started into growth. The soil needs to be kept quite moist throughout this period.

Once a few leaves have appeared bring the box into a light place. No artificial heat will be needed but they do need to be kept indoors until all danger of frost is passed. Harden off gradually.

FUCHSIAS

Autumn Remove the plants from their Summer containers and pot up into 15–22½cm (6–9") pots. Don't forget to label them. Keep in a frost-free greenhouse, shed or loft over the Winter. Gradually reduce their water supply until their leaves drop off. The plants need hardly any water from now until early Spring.

Spring Prune back the old wood to within two or three leaf nodes of the old season's growth. When new signs of life appear, this is the time to water again. By mid May the plants will be ready to be hardened off before being planted out for the Summer.

GERANIUMS

Autumn Take them out of their Summer containers, cut the top growth back to 10–15cm (4–6"), remove any remaining leaves and trim the roots. Label them, and plant individually in John Innes No 2 in a 10cm (4") pot. Keep them in a frost free but light position such as a window sill inside the house. Or if you have a large number to keep, you could place

them in a box of peat-based compost, packed closely together and put them in the garage, if it has light, or any other frost free place. Either way, water well when you first pot them up and then only water when absolutely necessary. You will recognize when the time has come when the new leaves begin to flag – it may only be necessary twice a month.

There may be other successful methods to keep geraniums but this way the old leaves, which may be harbouring rust and whitefly, will be stripped off leaving the new plants clean. Also the new growth which will be made in the late Autumn will be hardier than the old Summer growth which you have removed. By trimming the roots you will encourage new root hairs to grow which will strengthen the plant ready for when growth really gets going in the Spring. By then you should have good plants which will make rapid progress before you plant them out again in the Summer. This way you will also have been able to multiply from cuttings in the Spring.

Spring When new growth begins gradually increase the water supply. Take cuttings, and put them in 7½cm (3") pots full of John Innes seed compost. Harden off plants gradually before end May when they can take up their Summer residences.

LILIES

Autumn The old growth has to die down completely to ensure a good plant for next year therefore premature lifting would not be advised unless the lily could be transferred to the garden where the natural dying off process could continue.

Late Winter – early Spring On buying new bulbs plant them up individually into 15cm (6") pots of John Innes No 1. Keep in a cool dark place until top growth shows, when they can be brought into the daylight and given more moisture. By mid May they should have made a good start and be ready to plant out in a Summer scheme.

SPIDER PLANTS, MOTHER OF THOUSANDS, TRADESCANTIA, AND ORNAMENTAL ASPARAGUS

Autumn These can all be saved for the following year by potting up into 10–15cm (4–6") pots and placed on a light windowsill away from any danger of frost. You may like to increase your stock by taking cuttings from the tradescantia and potting up the runners from the spider plant and mother of thousands. The young plants will make good growth in the Spring and will soon be big enough to make a good display on their own.

HANGING BASKETS

101 A KALANCHOE HANGING BASKET

If you have a conservatory, you can enjoy this lovely hanging basket from April onwards. We bought these plants in flower in early April and the kalanchoe continued flowering for months. Towards the end of June we hung the basket outdoors where it flourished, its dainty little bells never failing to cause comment.

Site
In a conservatory from late Spring to early Summer; towards the end of June move to a sheltered sunny position outside.

Container
Wire hanging basket: 30 cm (12″) in diameter, with a 22½cm (9″) bracket.

Plant
In April if you have a sunroom or conservatory. Alternatively you could buy the plants later, keep them on a sunny windowsill and then make up the basket in mid June.

In flower
From time of purchase.

Ingredients
2 *Columnea* x *banksii* 'Variegata' with long pendulous stems, and with neat variegated leaves.
2 *Kalanchoe* 'Tessa', a bushy succulent with very dainty salmon pink pendulous flowers.
10 litres John Innes No 2 soil.
2 handfuls of grit.
1 basketful moss, sphagnum (preferably), ordinary wreath moss from a florists shop, or thick lawn moss.
Circle of plastic sheeting cut from a strong plastic bag, about the size of a dinner plate.

Method
1. Line the basket with a generous thickness of moss, starting at the base and working up the sides so that you form a collar above the rim of the basket.
2. Cut four 2½cm (1″) slits in the plastic circle and place over the moss lining in the bottom of the basket.
3. Spread two handfuls of grit over the plastic circle and then add 7½cm (3″) soil.
4. Arrange all the plants in the top of the basket so that they alternate and look well balanced. Make sure they are firmly in place, and then fill in the gaps with soil.
5. Water it well.

Aftercare
Water generously. In hot weather that means daily. Give a weekly liquid feed while flowering lasts.

Dismantle the basket in late Summer and pot the plants up in John Innes No 2. Keep them in a conservatory or on a sunny windowsill.

102 SOW A SWEET PEA HANGING BASKET

The seeds were sown in March without the help of artificial heat and by July the basket was looking a real picture and producing a wonderful scent.

Site
Sunny.

Container
Wire hanging basket: 35cm (14″) in diameter with a sturdy 27½cm (11″) bracket.

Early preparation
Sow the sweet pea seeds in early March as directed on the packet, or sow ten of them into one 7½cm (3″) deep tray or other container which is about the same width as the basket.

Plant
Make up the basket in the middle of May.

In flower
Mid June to end September.

Ingredients
10 dwarf sweet pea plants *Lathyrus odoratus* 'Bijou Mixed', 30cm (12″); there are many dwarf forms to choose from.
 1 pink verbena *Verbena* x *hybrida*.
 2 strips of lobelia, one blue and one mixed *Lobelia erinus* 'Sapphire' and 'String of Pearls'.
10 litres John Innes No 2 soil.
 2 handfuls of grit.
A basketful of moss, sphagnum (preferably) or ordinary wreath moss from a florists shop, or thick lawn moss.
Circle of plastic sheeting cut from a strong plastic bag, about the size of a dinner plate.

Method
1. Line the basket with a generous thickness of moss, starting at the base and working up the sides so that you form a collar above the rim of the basket.
2. Cut four 2½cm (1″) slits in the plastic circle and place over the moss lining in the bottom of the basket.
3. Spread two handfuls of grit over the plastic circle and then add 7½cm (3″) soil.
4. Gently divide the strips of lobelia, and plant from the outside of the basket inwards. Pass the roots through a hole you have made in the moss, about half way down the sides of the basket, so that they make good contact with the soil. Close the gap in the moss and continue round the basket. Use one strip for the middle and save the other for the top, but mix the different kinds if you like.
5. Plant the sweet peas in the top of the basket. If you have grown them all in one container so much the better as there will be less disturbance around their roots.
6. Plant the verbena at the back of the basket.
7. Plant the remaining lobelia around the rim.
8. Make sure that all the plants are firmly in place, filling any remaining gaps with soil.
9. Add more moss if necessary to make a thick collar at the top of the basket. This is important as it helps to retain the soil.
10. Water well. Add more soil if necessary.

Aftercare
Water generously. In hot weather you must be prepared to do it daily, but do not pour all the water on at once. Water, wait for it to soak in and then pour some more on.

Give a weekly liquid feed once flowering has begun. Spray for greenfly, etc as a matter of habit once a week as well. Deadhead regularly so that the sweet peas do not go to seed.

At the end of the Summer dismantle the basket and throw away all the plants.

103 A BASKET OF MORNING GLORY

We thought we had planted all blue morning glory!
Never mind, crimson mixed with blue still makes
quite a picture.

Site
Full sun.

Container
Wire hanging basket: 35cm (14″) in diameter with a
sturdy 27½cm (11″) bracket. This one is particularly
elegant.

Plant
June, but buy the geraniums and ground ivy in May.

In flower
It should begin to look good from end June onwards,
getting to its peak at end July early August.

Ingredients
  2 strips of white lobelia *Lobelia erinus* 'White Lady'.
  3 trailing ivy leaf geraniums: 2 white *Pelargonium*
     'Snow Queen' and 1 pink 'Apricot Queen'.
  3 upright geraniums: 2 carmine *Pelargonium* 'Polka'
     and 1 pink 'Party Dress'.
  5 morning glory *Ipomoea*, use 'Heavenly Blue' in
     preference.
  1 *Helichrysum petiolatum* 'Variegatum'.
  3 variegated ground ivies *Glechoma hederacea*
     'Variegata'.
10 litres John Innes No 2 soil.
  2 handfuls of grit.
A basketful of moss, sphagnum (preferably) or ordin-
    ary wreath moss from a florists shop, or thick
    lawn moss.
A circle of plastic sheeting cut from a strong plastic
    bag, about the size of a dinner plate.

Method
  1. Line the basket with a generous thickness of
     moss, starting at the base and working half way
     up the sides.
  2. Cut four 2½cm (1″) slits in the plastic circle
     and place over the moss lining in the bottom of
     the basket.
  3. Spread two handfuls of grit over the plastic
     circle and then add 7½cm (3″) soil.
  4. Take three of the morning glory and plant them
     through the wires at the side of the basket. You

may have to prize the wires open and close them again afterwards.

5. Gently divide one strip of lobelia, and plant it too around the middle of the basket. Make sure the roots make good contact with the soil.

6. Now add more moss, packing it tightly on top of the plants and bringing it right to the top so that it forms a collar above the rim of the basket.

7. Plant the trailing pink geranium in the centre front with two ground ivies either side. Then plant the two white trailing geraniums behind the ground ivy. Plant the third ground ivy at the back of the basket.

8. Fill in around the edge with lobelia.

9. Plant the upright pink geranium in the centre back of the basket with the helichrysum in front.

10 Plant the other two morning glory and the two 'Polka' geraniums on either side.

11 Make sure the container looks well balanced and that all the plants are firmly in place, filling any remaining gaps with soil.

12. Water well. Add more soil and moss around the top if necessary.

Aftercare
Once the morning glory gets established it will grow very quickly. Aim to get each of the side plants trailing down the ground ivies and the ones in the top climbing up the wires.

Water generously; in hot weather you must be prepared to do it daily. I find that about four litres (one gallon) is about right for a mature basket. But you can't just stand there and pour it all on. Pour some onto the top of the basket and then wait for it to soak in. Then pour some more on and wait for that to soak in. Too much too quickly will just result in it running all over the sides and washing the soil away with it. Your aim is to get the whole basket thoroughly wet so that the moss is wet to touch all the way round.

After mid July give a liquid feed once a fortnight. Spray for greenfly, etc as necessary. At the end of the Summer you should dismantle the basket. You can keep the geraniums indoors (see page 127). You may be able to keep the ground ivies outdoors if it is a mild Winter but discard the lobelia, morning glory and helichrysum.

104 A FOLIAGE BASKET

Here is something which is a little bit different. Not so much a flowering basket as a foliage basket where we can appreciate some of the interesting leaves which our Summer plants so often display.

Site
Sun or partial shade.

Container
Wire hanging basket: 35cm (14″) in diameter, with a sturdy 27½cm (11″) bracket.

Plant
Mid to end May (unless you have a greenhouse or conservatory in which case plant from mid April and keep it inside until end May).

In flower
It will provide interest as soon as you plant it and continue to do so until the end of September.

Ingredients
2 part strips of upright lobelia *Lobelia erinus* 'Mrs Clibran'; in late Summer her leaves turn bronze, and 'White Lady'.

2 variegated cream and purple ivy leaf geraniums *Pelargonium* 'L'elegante'.

1 green and gold cobweb marked ivy leaf geranium *Pelargonium* 'White Mesh'.

1 upright variegated scented leaf geranium *Pelargonium* 'Lady Plymouth'.

1 pink verbena *Verbena* x *hybrida* with the same colour flowers as the 'White Mesh' geranium.

2 mother of thousands which bears young plants on its runners, you can just see them already in the photograph *Saxifraga stolonifera* 'Tricolor'.

1 variegated spider plant which will also bear young plants on its runners. *Chlorophytum comosum* 'Mandaianum'.

2 coleus with their rich colouring in the leaves *Coleus blumei*.

10 litres John Innes No 2 soil.

2 handfuls of grit.

A basketful of moss, sphagnum (preferably), ordinary wreath moss from a florists shop, or thick lawn moss.

Circle of plastic sheeting cut from a strong plastic bag, about the size of a dinner plate.

Method

1. Line the basket with a generous thickness of moss, start at the base and work up the sides so that you form a collar above the rim of the basket.
2. Cut four 2½cm (1″) slits in the plastic circle and place over the moss lining in the bottom of the basket.
3. Spread two handfuls of grit over the plastic circle and then add 5cm (2″) soil.
4. Gently divide the 'Mrs Clibran' lobelia, and planting from the outside of the basket inwards, pass the roots through a hole you have made in the moss at the front of the basket, so that they make good contact with the soil. Close the gap in the moss and continue around the front of the basket.
5. Plant the 'White Mesh' geranium in the centre front of the basket with the two saxifrages tucked in on either side.
6. Plant the two 'L'Elegante' geraniums at the sides of the basket, behind the saxifrages.
7. Plant the 'Lady Plymouth' geranium in the centre with the verbena and spider plant at the back.
8. Tuck the white lobelia around the front rim of the basket.
9. Make sure the container looks well balanced and that all the plants are firmly in place, filling any remaining gaps with soil.
10. Water well. Add more soil or moss if necessary.

Aftercare

Water generously. In hot weather you must be prepared to do it daily. I find that about four litres (one gallon) is about right for a mature basket. In mid July give a liquid feed.

Spray for greenfly etc as a matter of habit once a week, and deadhead all fading geranium and verbena flowers regularly.

At the end of the Summer you should dismantle the basket. You can bring the geraniums, spider plant and mother of thousands indoors (see page 127), but discard the rest.

105 PETUNIAS AND 'MEXICANA' IN A HANGING BASKET

This soon creates a dazzling display, with its stripes and frills.

Site
Sunny.

Container
Wire hanging basket: 35cm (14″) in diameter, with a sturdy 27½cm (11″) bracket.

Plant
Mid to end May (unless you have a greenhouse or conservatory, in which case plant in mid April and keep it inside until end May).

In flower
From time of planting until end September.

Ingredients
  2 strips of trailing lobelia *Lobelia erinus* 'White Lady'.
  4 trailing ivy leaf geraniums *Pelargonium* 'Mexicana'.
  2 silver leaf cinerarias *Senecio cineraria* (*Cineraria maritima*).
  5 petunias *Petunia* x *hybrida*, Grandiflora type, of which 3 blue and white, 2 pink and white.
10 litres John Innes No 2 soil.
  2 handfuls of grit.
A basketful moss, sphagnum (preferably) or ordinary wreath moss from a florists shop, or thick lawn moss.
A circle of plastic sheeting cut from a strong plastic bag, about the size of dinner plate.

Method
1. Line the basket with a generous thickness of moss, starting at the base and working up the sides so that you form a collar above the rim of the basket.
2. Cut four 2½cm (1″) slits in the plastic circle and place over the moss lining in the bottom of the basket.
3. Spread two handfuls of grit over the plastic circle and then add 7½cm (3″) soil.
4. Gently divide the strips of lobelia, and aim to plant a circle around the middle of the basket. Starting from the outside of the basket inwards, pass the roots through a hole you have made in the moss so that they make good contact with the soil. Close the gap in the moss and continue round the basket. Use one strip for the middle round and another strip for the top.
5. Plant the four 'Mexicana' geraniums around the top of the basket, two at the front and two at the sides. Avoid the back as that will be hidden against the wall.
6. Then plant the second strip of lobelia around the top of the basket between the geraniums.
7. Make sure that all the plants are firmly in place, filling any remaining gaps with soil.
9. Water well. Add more soil or moss if necessary.

Aftercare
Water generously. In hot weather you must be prepared to do it daily. I find that four litres (roughly a gallon) is about right for a mature basket: first pour some of the water onto the top of the basket, and wait for it to soak in. Then pour some more on and wait for that to soak in. Your aim is to get the whole basket thoroughly wet so that the moss is wet to the touch all the way round.

Once a week give a liquid feed. Deadhead fading petunia and geranium flowers daily. Spray for greenfly, etc as a matter of routine once a week as well.

At the end of the Summer you should dismantle the basket. You can keep the geraniums (see page 127), but discard the rest.

106 THE TRADITIONAL MIX

This is the traditional mix in a hanging basket. Fuchsias, geraniums, busy lizzies, petunias and lobelia all combine to make a delightful display.

Site
Partial shade.

Container
Wire hanging basket: 35cm (14″) in diameter, with a sturdy 27½cm (11″) bracket.

Plant
Mid to end May (unless you have a greenhouse or conservatory in which case plant from mid April and keep it inside until end May).

In flower
It should begin to look good from mid June onwards.

Ingredients
  2 strips of trailing white lobelia *Lobelia erinus* 'White Lady'.
  3 blue and white trailing fuchsias *Fuchsia* 'Ed Lagerde'.
  2 trailing ivy leaf geraniums *Pelargonium* 'Achievement'.
  1 upright pink geranium *Pelargonium* 'Party Dress'.
  2 pink busy lizzies *Impatiens* F1 hybrids.
  2 dark blue petunias *Petunia* x *hybrida*, Grandiflora type.
 10 litres John Innes No 2 soil.
  2 handfuls of grit.
A basketful of moss, sphagnum (preferably), ordinary wreath moss from a florists, or thick lawn moss.
A circle of plastic sheeting cut from a strong plastic bag, about the size of a dinner plate.

Method
  1. Line the basket with a generous thickness of moss, starting at the base and working up the sides so that you form a collar above the rim.
  2. Cut four 2½cm (1″) slits in the plastic circle and place this over the moss lining in the bottom of the basket.
  3. Spread two handfuls of grit over the plastic circle and then add 7½cm (3″) soil.
  4. Gently divide the strip of lobelia, and planting from the outside of the basket inwards, pass the roots through a hole you have made in the moss, somewhere around the middle of the basket, so

that they make good contact with the soil. Close the gap in the moss and continue round the basket using half the lobelia.
  5. Plant the biggest fuchsia in the centre front of the basket so that it will eventually trail down the middle. Plant one 'Achievement' geranium and another fuchsia on either side.
  6. Plant the 'Party Dress' geranium in the centre back of the basket.
  7. Then plant the petunias and busy lizzies opposite one another in the middle of the basket.
  8. Tuck the rest of the lobelia around the front edge.
  9. Make sure the container looks well balanced and that all the plants are firmly in place, filling any remaining gaps with soil.
 10. Water well. Add more soil and moss if necessary.

Aftercare
Water generously. In hot weather you must be prepared to do it daily. Your aim is to get the whole basket thoroughly wet.

After mid July give an occasional liquid feed. Spray for greenfly, etc once a week and deadhead all fading flowers regularly. At the end of the Summer you should dismantle the basket. You can keep the geraniums and fuchsias indoors (see page 127), but discard the rest.

107 AN ALL WHITE HANGING BASKET

In really hot weather this still manages to look cool and refreshing. Then in the evening it becomes almost luminous as the end of the day approaches and the light gets dimmer.

Site
On a partly shaded wall.

Container
Wire hanging basket: 35cm (14″) in diameter, with a sturdy 27½cm (11″) bracket.

Early preparation
Follow the instructions on page 127 if you wish to bring on your own begonia tubers.

Plant
Mid to end May (unless you have a greenhouse or conservatory in which case plant from mid April and keep it inside until end May).

In flower
It should begin to look good from mid June onwards.

Ingredients
2 strips of trailing white lobelia *Lobelia erinus* 'White Lady'.
2 white trailing ivy leaf geraniums *Pelargonium* 'Snow Queen'.
2 white upright single geraniums *Pelargonium* 'Immaculata'.
3 white trailing begonias *Begonia* x *tuberhybrida*.
2 white busy lizzies *Impatiens* F1 hybrids.
1 ornamental asparagus *Asparagus* 'Sprengeri'.
10 litres John Innes No 2 soil.
2 handfuls of grit.
A basketful of moss, sphagnum (preferably), ordinary wreath moss from a florists, or thick lawn moss.
A circle of plastic sheeting cut from a strong plastic bag, about the size of a dinner plate.

Method
1. Line the basket with a generous thickness of moss, starting at the base and working up the sides so that you form a collar above the rim.
2. Cut four 2½cm (1″) slits in the plastic circle and place over the moss lining in the bottom of the basket.
3. Spread two handfuls of grit over the plastic circle and then add 5cm (2″) soil.

4. Gently divide the strip of lobelia. Make a hole in the moss in the centre of the basket and, planting from the outside of the basket inwards, pass the roots through into the centre of the basket, so that they make good contact with the soil. Close the gap in the moss and continue round the basket. Use one strip for the middle round and save the other strip for the top.
5. Plant the biggest of the three begonias in the centre front of the basket and, leaving a small gap, plant the other two on either side.
6. Plant the two 'Snow Queen' geraniums in between the begonias.
7. Plant the two 'Immaculata' geraniums in the centre back of the basket.
8. Plant the asparagus towards the front of the basket with the two busy lizzies on either side.
9. Make sure that all the plants are firmly in place, filling any remaining gaps with soil.
10. Water well. Add more soil and moss if necessary.

Aftercare
Water generously. In hot weather you must be prepared to do it daily.

Give a liquid feed once a fortnight and spray for greenfly, etc once a week. At the end of the Summer dismantle the basket. Keep the geraniums, asparagus and begonias (see page 127), but discard the rest.

108 ORANGE AND PINK IN A HANGING BASKET

Brilliant oranges, and pale pinks are sure to enliven any dull spot, and this basket will certainly tolerate shade.

Site
In full or partial shade.

Container
Wire hanging basket: 35cm (14″) in diameter, with a sturdy 27½cm (11″) bracket.

Early preparation
Follow the instructions on page 127 if you wish to start your own begonia tubers

Plant
Mid to end May (unless you have a greenhouse or conservatory in which case plant from mid April and keep it inside until end May).

In flower
It should begin to look good from mid June onwards.

Ingredients
1 strip upright lobelia *Lobelia erinus* 'Mrs Clibran'.
1 orange non-stop begonia *Begonia* x *tuberhybrida*.
3 orange trailing begonias *Begonia* x *tuberhybrida*.
1 large orange or salmon pink fuchsia *Fuchsia* 'Orange Drops'.
3 pink busy lizzies *Impatiens* F1 hybrids.
2 tradescantia or wandering jew *Tradescantia albiflora*.
10 litres John Innes No 2 soil or a peat-based compost.
2 handfuls of grit.
A basketful of moss, sphagnum (preferably), ordinary wreath moss from a florists shop, or thick lawn moss.
A circle of plastic sheeting cut from a strong plastic bag, about the size of a dinner plate.

Method
1. Line the basket with a generous thickness of moss, starting at the base and working up the sides so that you form a collar above the rim of the basket.
2. Cut four 2½cm (1″) slits in the plastic circle and place over the moss lining in the bottom of the basket.
3. Spread two handfuls of grit over the plastic circle and then add 7½cm (3″) soil.
4. Gently divide the strip of lobelia. Make a hole in the moss in the centre of the basket and planting from the outside of the basket inwards, pass the roots through the moss until they make good contact with the soil. Close the gap in the moss and continue round the middle of the basket.
5. Plant the largest of the three trailing begonias at the front of the basket, leave a gap and then plant the other two on either side.
6. Plant the fuchsia in the middle and the non-stop begonia towards centre back.
7. Plant the three busy lizzies behind the trailing begonias.
8. Tuck the tradescantia between the busy lizzies.
9. Make sure the container looks well balanced and that all the plants are firmly in place, filling any remaining gaps with soil.
10. Water well. Add more soil or moss if necessary.

Aftercare
Water generously. In hot weather you must be prepared to do it daily. We find that four litres (one gallon) is about right for a mature basket. Use a long spouted watering-can so that you can water under the leaves at soil level. Otherwise the water will just run off the leaves and on to the ground.

Once a week give a liquid feed. Spray for greenfly, etc as necessary and deadhead all fading begonia and fuchsia flowers.

At the end of the Summer you should dismantle the basket. You can keep the fuchsia, and the begonias (see page 127) over the Winter. Take cuttings of the tradescantia if you like and grow them indoors but throw the lobelia away.

109 UNRULY BUT COLOURFUL

The basket is teaming with bright fiery colours. If you can put up with unruly nasturtiums, they can be very rewarding.

Site
Sun or light shade.

Container
Wire hanging basket: 35cm (14″) with a sturdy 27½cm (11″) bracket.

Early preparation
You should sow the nasturtiums in March as directed on the packet. If you want to bring on your own begonias see page 127.

Plant
Mid to end May.

In flower
It should begin to look good from mid June onwards.

Ingredients
6 nasturtium plants either bought, or raised from seed *Tropaeolum* 'Double Gleam Mixed', 30cm (12″) long, semi-trailing, semi-double and sweetly scented.
2 calceolarias or slipper flowers *Calceolaria integrifolia,* height about 30cm (12″).
3 orange trailing begonias, *Begonia* x *tuberhybrida*.
2 red busy lizzies *Impatiens* F1 hybrids.
10 litres John Innes No 2 soil.
2 handfuls of grit.
A basketful of moss, sphagnum (preferably), ordinary wreath moss from a florists shop, or thick lawn moss.
A circle of plastic sheeting cut from a strong plastic bag, about the size of a dinner plate.

Method
1. Line the basket with a generous thickness of moss, starting at the base and working up the sides so that you form a collar above the rim of the basket.
2. Cut four 2½cm (1″) slits in the plastic circle and place this over the moss lining in the bottom of the basket.
3. Spread two handfuls of grit over the plastic circle and then add 7½cm (3″) soil. Plant the biggest of the three begonias at the centre front of the basket with the other two on either side.
4. Plant the two busy lizzies towards the centre back of the basket along with the two calceolarias.
5. Plant the six nasturtiums to the front and sides of the basket.
6. Make sure the plants are firmly in place, filling any remaining gaps with soil.
7. Water well. Add more soil and moss if necessary.

Aftercare
Water generously. In hot weather you must be prepared to do it daily. Give an occasional liquid feed once the nasturtiums have begun to flower. Don't over do it though or the nasturtiums will go rampant with leaves rather than flowers.

Spray for blackfly as soon as they appear on the nasturtiums – as they surely will. At the end of the Summer you should dismantle the basket. You can keep the begonias (see page 127), but discard the rest.

110 EXTRA DAINTY

These pale pink fuchsias and geraniums make a dainty display against the trailing ground ivy.

Site
In partial shade.

Container
Wire hanging basket: 30cm (12″) in diameter, with a sturdy 22½cm (9″) bracket.

Plant
Mid to end May (unless you have a greenhouse or conservatory in which case plant from mid April and keep it inside until end May).

In flower
It should begin to look good from mid June onwards.

Ingredients
  2 strips of trailing lobelia *Lobelia erinus* 'Blue Cascade'.
  3 pale pink trailing fuchsias *Fuchsia* 'Sophisticated Lady'.
  3 scented leaf geraniums of which 2 *Pelargonium* 'Sweet Mimosa', 1 *Pelargonium* 'Lady Plymouth'.
  3 variegated ground ivies *Glechoma hederacea* 'Variegata'.
10 litres John Innes No 2 soil.
  2 handfuls of grit.
A basketful of moss, sphagnum, ordinary wreath moss from a florists shop, or thick lawn moss.
A circle of plastic sheeting cut from a strong plastic bag, about the size of a dinner plate.

Method
1. Line the basket with a generous thickness of moss, starting at the base and working up the sides so that you form a collar above the rim of the basket.
2. Cut four 2½cm (1″) slits in the plastic circle and place this over the moss lining in the bottom of the basket.
3. Spread two handfuls of grit over the plastic circle and then add 7½cm (3″) soil.
4. Gently divide one strip of lobelia and, planting from the outside of the basket inwards, pass the roots through a hole you have made in the moss in the centre of the basket so that they make good contact with the soil. Close the gap in the moss and continue round the basket.
5. Plant the biggest fuchsia in the centre front of the basket, and leave a gap before planting the other two on either side.
6. Plant the three ground ivies close to the fuchsias.
7. Plant the two 'Sweet Mimosa' geraniums behind the front ground ivies.
8. Divide the second strip of lobelia and plant it around the rim of the basket.
9. Make sure the container looks well balanced and that all the plants are firmly in place, filling any remaining gaps with soil.
10. Water well. Add soil and moss if necessary.

Aftercare
Water generously. In hot weather you must be prepared to do it daily.

Give a liquid feed at the beginning of July and August. Deadhead all fading flowers. Spray for greenfly, etc as a matter of habit once a week as well.

At the end of the Summer, dismantle the basket. You can keep the geraniums, and the fuchsias (see page 127), and in sheltered areas the ground ivy may survive outdoors, but discard the lobelia.

111 A BALL OF BUSY LIZZIES

This is a good basket for sun or shade and the colours can be varied to suit yourself. It is easy to look after.

Site
It will enjoy the sun and tolerate quite deep shade.

Container
Wire hanging basket: 30cm (12″) in diameter, with a sturdy 22½cm (9″) bracket.

Plant
Mid to end May.

In flower
It should begin to look good from mid June onwards.

Ingredients
9 busy lizzies *Impatiens* F1 hybrids, any mixture of colours.
2 strips of trailing lobelia *Lobelia erinus* 'String of Pearls'.
10 litres John Innes No 2 soil or a peat-based compost.
2 handfuls of grit.
A basketful of moss, sphagnum (preferably), ordinary wreath moss from a florists, or thick lawn moss.
A circle of plastic sheeting cut from a strong plastic bag, about the size of a dinner plate.

Method
1. Line the basket with a generous thickness of moss, starting at the base and working one third of the way up the sides.
2. Cut four 2½cm (1″) slits in the plastic circle and place over the moss lining in the bottom of the basket.
3. Spread two handfuls of grit over the plastic circle and then add 5cm (2″) soil.
4. Gently divide one strip of lobelia and, planting from the outside of the basket inwards, pass the roots between the wires so that they make good contact with the soil. Continue round the basket.
5. Add another ring of moss, compressing it downwards so that there are no gaps around the lobelia plants.
6. Plant four busy lizzies at regular intervals around the front and sides of the basket (only avoid the back as this will be against the wall). If necessary force the wires open to pass the roots through and then close them again afterwards.

7. Add more soil so that the roots of the busy lizzies are covered.
8. Add another ring of moss, bringing it right to the top so that it forms a good thick collar 2½cm (1″) above the rim of the basket.
9. Plant the remaining busy lizzies in the top of the basket.
10. Carefully divide the second strip of lobelia and plant around the rim so that it will trail over the sides.
11. Make sure the container looks well balanced and that all the plants are firmly in place, filling any remaining gaps with soil.
12. Water carefully but well. Add more soil and moss if necessary.

Aftercare
Water generously. In hot weather you must be prepared to do it daily, if not twice a day. But take your time. Too much water too quickly will just result in it running all over the sides and washing the soil away with it. Your aim is to get the whole basket thoroughly wet so that the moss is wet to touch all the way round.

Once a week give the plants a liquid feed. At the end of Summer dismantle the basket and discard all the plants.

112 A BASKET OF SWEET PEAS

Imagine the wonderful scent from these dwarf sweet peas as they tumble out of their wicker basket. They make a very pretty picture and would be an unusual present.

Site
Sunny position.

Container
This is an old wicker basket: 15cm (6″) deep, 25cm (10″) wide, 30cm (12″) long. Almost any wicker basket will do. However, it is vital that it receives three good coats of yacht varnish to preserve it out of doors.

Early preparation
These sweet peas are not easily obtainable so you will have to buy the seeds and plant them in early March. If you want this particular alyssum you will need to grow it from seed as well; otherwise, you will be able to buy pink alyssum easily in May.

In flower
End June to September.

Ingredients
4 dwarf sweet pea seedlings *Lathyrus odoratus* 'Pink Cupid'. This one is especially fragrant and very neat in habit.
9 plants or 1 strip pink alyssum *Lobularia maritima* 'Wonderland'.
6 litres John Innes No 2 soil.
Small pieces of polystyrene to use for drainage.
Black plastic sheeting to use as a liner.

Method
1. Cut some black plastic sheeting to fit inside the basket and make six 2½cm (1″) slits along the bottom area to provide drainage holes.
2. Put 2½cm (1″) drainage material on top of the lining and cover this with soil so that it reaches just below the rim of the basket. Firm the soil down gently.
3. Plant two sweet peas on each side of the basket.
4. Take the alyssum and, carefully separating the individual plants, set them around the edge of the basket.
5. Make sure that all the plants are firmly in place.
6. Water well and place in a very sunny spot. It will be better if you can raise it slightly to stop water being trapped underneath.

Aftercare
They need moisture but be careful not to overwater. They will benefit from an occasional liquid feed. Spray against greenfly, etc as necessary.

Remove old flowers as they fade to prolong the period of bloom. At the end of the Summer all the contents should be discarded.

113 A BASKET OF ROSES

'Snowball' is a delightful miniature rose which looks lovely in this basket against a pretty frill of pale blue lobelia.

Site
Sunny position.

Container
An old wicker basket: 17½cm (7″) deep and 35cm (14″) long. It must be given three coats of yacht varnish to preserve it whilst outdoors.

Early preparation
Purchase as 'dry rootstock' in late Autumn or container grown in early Spring. Availability might be limited so it is best to order in advance from a rose specialist or from a good local garden centre. However, there is nothing to stop you using another variety of miniature rose: by early Summer the garden centres usually have a very good choice.

In flower
End June into July, then continuing throughout the Summer.

Ingredients
1 miniature rose *Rosa* 'Snowball', 15–20cm (6–8″) tall and 37½cm (15″) across.
1 strip of pale blue lobelia *Lobelia erinus* 'Cambridge Blue'.
7 litres John Innes No 3 soil.
Drainage material such as crocks or small pieces of polystyrene.
Black plastic sheeting to use as a lining for the basket.

Method
1. If you are planting a bare rootstock rose you should heel it into the garden as soon as you receive it, and then plant it up in the basket in March.
2. If you are using a container-grown rose, plant it in the basket on purchase either in the early Spring or early Summer.
3. Prepare the basket by lining it with black plastic sheeting which has six 2½cm (1″) slits along the bottom to provide for drainage.
4. Cover lining with 2½cm (1″) drainage material and add 5cm (2″) of soil.
5. Put the rose in the basket so that the union of the stock and scion is about 2½cm (1″) below the rim of the basket. If you are using an uncontainerised plant make sure that the roots are well spread before covering with soil.
6. Bring the soil level above the union so that it reaches within 1cm (½″) of the rim.
7. Firm the rose gently into the soil.
8. Water well and add more soil if necessary to regain the former level.
9. Trim off any pieces of black sheeting which are still exposed.
10. Keep the basket raised off the ground so that water doesn't collect underneath.
11. In the middle of May separate a strip of lobelia and plant six plants around the edge of the basket. Water well.

Aftercare
Take care to water the basket regularly so that the soil is never allowed to dry out. Foliar feeding is recommended in May, June and July. Look out for damage by insects and pests and spray weekly.

During the main flowering period deadhead all faded flowers by cutting back as far as the first outward pointing leaf. As Summer progresses merely remove old flowers.

At the end of Autumn, remove the rose from the basket and plant in the garden. The basket will need another three coats of yacht varnish before it can be used again for another planting.

114 A BASKET OF BEGONIAS

Begonias make a stunning display in this basket. Once planted, they are simple to care for and will go on flowering for months.

Site
Begonias are not fussy and will thrive in sun or partial shade.

Container
A wicker or bamboo basket: 50cm (20″) long, 40cm (16″) wide, 15cm (6″) deep. It must be given three coats of yacht varnish to preserve it whilst outdoors. It has a lovely high handle which still shows above the display but by the end of Summer this will probably be hidden.

Plant
You can buy these plants in May, but if you want to grow them on yourself from tubers buy them in February or March at the latest. (See page 127.)

In flower
Early June until end September.

Ingredients
  4 non-stop begonias *Begonia* x *tuberhybrida.*
  1 strip of upright lobelia *Lobelia erinus* 'Mrs Clibran'; dark blue with white eye.
  ½ basketful sphagnum or ordinary wreath moss from a florist, if you have an open bamboo basket as shown above.
 12 litres of peat-based compost or John Innes No 2 soil.
  3 handfuls of grit.
Black plastic sheeting to line the basket.

Method
1. If you are using an open bamboo basket line it with a generous thickness of moss. Start at the base and bring it well up the sides to form a collar above the rim of the basket.
2. Whatever sort of basket you are using, cut six 2½cm (1″) slits in the plastic sheeting and line the base and sides.
3. Cover the lining with grit and add 5cm (2″) soil.
4. Remove the begonias from their pots, keeping their roots intact. If you have two smaller plants, place them together in the centre, leaving the bigger plants for either end of the basket.
5. Fill the gaps in between the plants with soil,

bringing the level to within 2½cm (1″) of the rim of the basket.
6. Carefully separate the strip of lobelia and plant it around the edge of the basket.
7. Water well, in between rather than on top of the plants. Add more soil if necessary to bring soil up to its former level.
8. Raise the basket off the ground so that water doesn't collect and stagnate underneath it.

Aftercare
The basket should be watered regularly as rain will run off the big begonia leaves and miss the soil. Use a long spouted watering can so that you can get between the plants, and water either in the morning or late evening to avoid scorching the leaves.

Once flowering has begun, give the plants a liquid feed every two weeks. At the same time check for insect damage to the lobelia and spray if necessary.

By Autumn the begonia leaves will begin to turn yellow. Bring the basket indoors so that the tubers are not damaged by frost and allow them to dry out completely by gradually reducing their supply of water.

Remove the tubers from the basket and overwinter them in a cool, frost-free environment 7–10°C (45–50°F), covered with peat.

The whole process of growth can then begin again in late Winter. The lobelia cannot be kept for another year and should be discarded.

WINDOW BOXES

115 COLOURFUL ANTIRRHINUMS

Dwarf antirrhinums make a pretty show in a window box although you will have to wait until July to see them at their best.

Site
Sunny window ledge.

Container
Large terracotta window box: 80cm (32″) long, 20cm (8″) wide, 17½cm (7″) deep.

Early preparation
Sow the antirrhinums in early Spring. They are easy to germinate and look after. Alternatively, they are readily available as seedlings in May although the dwarf varieties are not so easy to find.

Plant
Mid to end May.

In flower
July to August.

Ingredients
1 strip or 7 plants of dwarf antirrhinum or snap-dragon *Antirrhinum majus* 'F1 Floral Carpet Mixed'.
½ strip of white alyssum *Lobularia maritima* 'Little Dorrit'.
25 litres John Innes No 2 soil.
Grit or small pieces of polystyrene as drainage material.

Method
1. Cover the base of the container with 2½cm (1″) drainage material and add 12½cm (5″) soil.
2. Carefully separate the strip of antirrhinums, and choose the seven best plants.
3. Space them along the centre of the box.
4. Divide the half strip of alyssum and use as an edging around the front of the box.
5. Make sure that all the plants are firmly in place, filling any remaining gaps with soil.
6. Water well. Add more soil if necessary.
7. Pinch out the growing points of all the antirrhinums to encourage a bushy shape (check to see if it's been done already although this is doubtful).

Aftercare
Water regularly and give a liquid feed every two weeks from mid July. Discard all plants at the end of the flowering period.

116 UNIQUE

Soft grey, yellow and burnt orange are not easy colours for a Summer planting. However, by the careful use of foliage as well as flowers, we are able to complement the beautiful marbling on the box. It illustrates the importance of colour-scheme and balance.

Site
Window ledge in sun or partial shade.

Container
Large window box (marble painting on wood): 105cm (42″) long, 20cm (8″) wide, 25cm (10″) deep.

Early preparation (optional for the lilies and begonias.)
1. Buy the lilies in late Winter and plant singly in 15cm (6″) pots using John Innes No 1 soil.
2. Buy the begonia tubers in February and begin growth by early March (see page 127).
3. Sow the nasturtium seeds in early March, following the instructions on the packet. You will find it difficult to buy this variety as growing plants, so try and send away for the seeds in late Winter.

Plant
End May.

In flower
June to October.

Ingredients
2 *Perilla frutescens* with its dark red foliage.
2 short yellow lilies *Lilium* 'Sunray'.
6 dwarf yellow nasturtiums *Tropaeolum* 'Peach Melba'.
4 dwarf bedding dahlias bought with the colours already showing; 2 yellow, 2 orange-red.
5 non-stop begonias; 2 yellow, 3 orange *Begonia* x *tuberhybrida*.
3 *Sedum sieboldii* 'Mediovariegatum'; spread up to 37½cm (15″), used as a foliage plant.
2 *Senecio cineraria* (*Cineraria maritima*) 'Silver Dust', again used only for the foliage effect.
50 litres John Innes No 2 soil.
Drainage material such as crocks or pieces of broken polystyrene.

Method
1. Cover the base of the container with 2½cm (1″) drainage material and add 7½cm (3″) soil.
2. Plant the perillas at either end towards the back of the box with a nasturtium just in front.
3. Working inwards still towards the back, plant an orange begonia and a yellow lily at either end.
4. Along the front of the box from left to right, plant a yellow dahlia, nasturtium, silver cineraria, sedum, nasturtium, another sedum for the centre, then a nasturtium, sedum, silver cineraria, nasturtium, and lastly a second yellow dahlia.
5. In the centre of the box, behind the sedum, plant the third orange begonia.
6. Plant the two remaining nasturtiums at the back of the box on either side of the centre.
7. The exact positions are not crucial as long as the container is well balanced both in terms of colour arrangement and height.
8. Make sure all the plants are firmly in place, filling any remaining gaps with soil.
9. Water well. Add more soil if necessary.

Aftercare
This is a thirsty box and needs watering regularly, even daily in hot weather. Do not water in full sun but wait until early morning or evening. Give a liquid feed once a week.

Watch out for blackfly on the nasturtiums, and greenfly generally. Spray accordingly. Deadhead all faded flowers.

After the flowering period is over, discard the silver cineraria, the nasturtiums, and the dahlias. If you have not already cut the tops off, transplant the lilies to another part of the garden. Lift, clean and store begonia tubers in peat (see page 127).

The sedum might survive a mild Winter left in a sheltered spot outdoors, otherwise pot it up and take it to a cool spot in the house.

117 SHADES OF SALMON, ORANGE AND YELLOW

This box is only 20cm (8") deep but it is packed with plants and overflowing with colour. You don't have to follow the recipe exactly to get good results.

Site
Window ledge, some sun.

Container
Large wooden window box: 82½cm (33") long, 20cm (8") wide, 20cm (8") deep.

Early preparation
Sow the nasturtium seeds in early March following the instructions on the packet. Either buy begonia tubers in February or buy the flowering plants in May.

Plant
Mid to end May.

In flower
June to September.

Ingredients
3 double fuchsias *Fuchsia* 'Gilda' with a large full flower and golden green foliage.
2 orange non-stop begonias *Begonia* x *tuberhybrida*.
2 orange trailing begonias *Begonia* x *tuberhybrida*.
3 salmon pink busy lizzies *Impatiens* F1 hybrid.
2 variegated ground ivies *Glechoma hederacea* 'Variegata'.
2 black-eyed Susans *Thunbergia alata* 'Susie Mixed'; these came from a mixed packet of seeds; one is white, the other yellow.
3 calceolaria or slipper flowers *Calceolaria integrifolia*, height about 30cm (12").
3 salmon pink semi-double upright Irene geraniums *Pelargonium* 'Springtime'.
2 red semi-double upright Irene geraniums *Pelargonium* 'Toyon'.
1 dwarf or semi-trailing nasturtium *Tropaeolum* 'Peach Melba', 22½cm (9") spread.
25 litres John Innes No 2 soil.
Drainage material such as small pieces of polystyrene.

Method
1. Cover the base of the container with 2½cm (1") drainage material and add 10cm (4") soil.
2. Plant the front of the box so that from left to right you have: a fuchsia, ground ivy, empty pot for the black-eyed Susan, trailing begonia, nasturtium, centre fuchsia, trailing begonia, another empty pot for the second black-eyed Susan, ground ivy, and the remaining fuchsia.
3. In the middle of the box, plant the two non-stop begonias behind the trailing begonias. Then in the centre and at both ends plant the busy lizzies.
4. At the back of the box and in each corner, plant a calceolaria. Then alternate the geraniums 'Springtime' and 'Toyon' with an additional calceolaria in the centre.
5. Make sure the container looks well balanced and that all the plants are firmly in place, filling any remaining gaps with soil.
6. Water well. Add more soil if necessary.
7. Remove the empty pots and plant the black-eyed Susans when they become available in July.

Aftercare
This window box needs to be kept well fed and watered as it is so full of plants. You will probably need to water daily and once flowering has begun feed weekly.

Watch out for whitefly and blackfly, etc especially on the calceolarias and the nasturtium. Spray as a matter of habit once a week. Deadhead faded flowers as soon as you can.

At the end of the flowering season discard the calceolarias and the nasturtium. You may keep the rest of the plants for another year (see page 127). The ground ivy might even survive outside in a mild Winter.

118 ALL SORTS OF EVERYTHING

We wanted to create something bright for a London basement where the colours would shout out and the plants would intermingle. There was to be no colour scheme, just an effect of abundant growth.

Site
Window ledge in partial shade.

Container
Large terracotta window box: 80cm (32″) long, 20cm (8″) wide, 17½cm (7″) deep.

Early preparation
Buy the begonia tubers in February and get them started into growth by early March (see page 127). You can buy the plants in May but the choice will be restricted and they will be more expensive.

Plant
Mid to end May.

In flower
June until end September.

Ingredients (for just one box)
3 double begonias, one yellow, two orange *Begonia* x *tuberhybrida*.
3 trailing begonias one yellow, two orange *Begonia* x *tuberhybrida*.
2 pink trailing ivy leaved geraniums *Pelargonium* 'Mme Crousse'.
2 yellow (or white) daisy-like marguerites *Chrysanthemum frutescens* 'Jamaica Primrose'.
2 red busy lizzies *Impatiens* F1 hybrids.
1 strip of trailing lobelia *Lobelia erinus* 'Blue Cascade'.
½ strip of white alyssum *Lobularia maritima*.
25 litres John Innes No 2 soil.
Drainage material such as small pieces of polystyrene.

Method
1. Cover the base of the container with 2½cm (1″) drainage material and add 7½cm (3″) soil.
2. Along the back of the box, from left to right, plant: an orange double begonia, a yellow marguerite, a yellow double begonia, a second yellow marguerite and a second orange double begonia.
3. Along the front of the box, from left to right, alternate the trailing begonias and geraniums. Fill in the gaps between these plants with lobelia and alyssum.
4. Plant the busy lizzies in the middle of the box on either side of centre.
5. Make sure that all the plants are firmly in place, filling any remaining gaps with soil.
6. Water well. Add more soil if necessary.

Aftercare
This is heavily planted as you can see and needs a plentiful supply of water. But on a sunny day only water in the early morning or evening or you will scorch the leaves.

Feed weekly from the end of June onward. Look out for greenfly, etc and also for chrysanthemum leaf miner maggots on the marguerites and spray accordingly. Deadhead regularly to prolong the flowering period.

Before the first frosts appear, pot up the begonias and geraniums and bring indoors (see page 127). Discard the lobelia, busy lizzies and marguerites.

119 ROBOT PAINTBOX

Bright and cheerful, like the curtains; this is an easy window box to plant, simple to look after and is perfect for a child's bedroom.

Site
Window ledge, sunny aspect.

Container
Medium wooden window box (with a plastic liner): 55cm (22″) long, 15cm (6″) wide, 12½cm (5″) deep.

Plant
Middle to end May.

In flower
June to September.

Ingredients
1 strip of dwarf French marigolds *Tagetes patula* 'Leopard', 20cm (8″) high.
1 strip of upright dark blue lobelia *Lobelia erinus* 'Crystal Palace'.
9 litres John Innes No 2 soil or a peat-based compost.
Drainage material such as broken pieces of polystyrene.

Method
1. Cover the base of the container with 2½cm (1″) drainage material and add enough soil to bring the level just below the rim of the box.
2. Carefully separate the tagetes, and plant them in two rows along the front and back of the box.
3. Now carefully separate the lobelia, and plant these in between the tagetes leaving two for either end of the box.
4. Make sure the container is well balanced and that all the plants are firmly in place.
5. Water well. Add more soil if necessary.

Aftercare
Window boxes get very little rain water, especially when they are full of dense foliage, so they need watering regularly. Lobelia, in particular, does not like being kept dry.

Only an occasional liquid feed is necessary. Deadheading the tagetes helps but is not vital. The plants should remain free from pests. At the end of the flowering season discard all the contents.

120 A WINDOW BOX OF GERANIUMS

This is a simple
arrangement of
geraniums and ageratum.

Site
Sunny.

Container
Small terracotta window
box: 35cm (14″) long,
17½cm (7″) wide, 15cm
(6″) deep.

Plant
Mid to end May.

In flower
June to end September.

Ingredients
2 soft pink, striped and feathered geraniums *Pelargonium* 'Queen of Hearts'.
2 carmine red geraniums *Pelargonium* 'Polka'.
½ strip of mid-blue ageratum *Ageratum houstonianum*.
10 litres John Innes No 2 soil.
Drainage material such as grit, crocks or small pieces of polystyrene.

Method
1. Cover the base of the container with drainage material and add 5cm (2″) of soil.
2. Plant the 'Queen of Hearts' towards the back of the box on either side of centre, with a 'Polka' in front.
3. Add soil around each plant bringing the level to within 2½cm (1″) of the rim.
4. Divide the ageratum and plant right at the front of the box so that it will form a good edge to the display.
5. Check to see that the container looks well balanced and firm down all the plants.
6. Water well and add more soil if necessary.

Aftercare
For the sake of the ageratum in particular, water regularly. Feed occasionally with a liquid fertilizer from the end of June onwards.

Remove dead flowers and spray for whitefly, etc as necessary. At the end of the flowering period discard the ageratum.

The geraniums should be over-wintered if possible as these are rather special ones. (See page 127).

121 A MID TO LATE SUMMER BOX

This is a bright and cheerful box of dahlias, calceolarias and lobelia to last from July until October.

Site
Window ledge, preferably in sun.

Container
Large terracotta window box: 80cm (32″) long, 20cm (8″) wide, 17½cm (7″) deep.

Early preparation
If you want to use collerette dahlias you should either buy the tubers in early Spring and place on top of moist peat to start them into growth. Otherwise buy them as growing plants in May.

Plant
In the window box at the end of May.

In flower
July to October.

Ingredients
3 dahlias; these are the collerette type and have orange red petals with a yellow collar.
2 calceolarias or slipper flowers *Calceolaria integrifolia*, height about 30cm (12″).
1 strip of dark blue lobelia *Lobelia erinus* 'Mrs Clibran'.
25 litres John Innes No 2 soil.
Drainage material such as small pieces of polystyrene.

Method
1. Cover the base of the container with 2½cm (1″) drainage material and add 5cm (2″) soil.

2. Plant the dahlias, one in the centre and one at each end of the box.
3. Plant the calceolarias in between the dahlias.
4. Carefully divide the strip of lobelia and plant along the front and sides of the box.
5. Make sure the container looks well balanced and that all the plants are firmly in place, filling any remaining gaps with soil.
6. Water well. Add more soil if necessary.

Aftercare
Pinch out the growing tip of the dahlias and calceolarias if it has not already been done. You will need to water regularly – they are thirsty drinkers and will soon wilt if they are dry. Feed occasionally once flowering has begun.

Spray for greenfly, etc once a week as a matter of routine, as both the dahlias and the calceolarias attract bugs of one sort or another! In the late Autumn, discard the lobelia and calceolarias.

The dahlia tubers may be saved for next year. Cut off the foliage to within 10cm (4″) of the soil level, lift, clean and store upside down for a week protected from any rain. Store through the Winter on top of peat in a shallow box at a temperature of 5°C (41°F).

122 AN ALL WHITE WINDOW BOX

This collection of white flowers creates an eye catching display, and provides a restful picture on a hot Summer afternoon.

Site
Window ledge in sun or partial shade.

Container
Large terracotta window box: 80cm (32″) long, 20cm (8″) wide, 17½cm (7″) deep.

Early preparation
Begonias can be bought as growing plants in May, but it is much cheaper to grow them yourself (see page 127).

Plant
End May.

In flower
End May to end Spetember.

Ingredients
2 white geraniums *Pelargonium* 'Immaculata'.
2 white daisy-like marguerites *Chrysanthemum frutescens*.
1 double white begonia *Begonia* x *tuberhybrida*.
2 white trailing begonias *Begonia* x *tuberhybrida*.
3 trailing white ivy-leaved geraniums *Pelargonium* 'L'elegante'.
½ strip of white alyssum *Lobularia maritima*.
25 litres John Innes No 2 soil or a peat-based compost.
Drainage material such as crocks or small pieces of polystyrene.

Method
1. Cover the base of the container with 2½cm (1″) drainage material and add 5cm (2″) soil.
2. Plant the three 'L'elegante' geraniums along the front of the box with the two trailing begonias in between.
3. Plant the two 'Immaculata' geraniums at either end of the box at the back.
4. Plant the double begonia in the middle at the back.
5. Plant the marguerites at either side of the double begonia.
6. Divide the alyssum and plant along the front of the box.
7. Make sure the container looks well balanced and that all the plants are firmly in place, filling any remaining gaps with soil.
8. Water well. Add more soil if necessary.

Aftercare
This represents a full planting and needs plenty of care as to watering.

Feed regularly once a week, and spray regularly for greenfly, etc. The marguerite may be attacked by chrysanthemum leaf miner and would need to be treated accordingly.

At the end of the Summer discard the marguerite and alyssum. If you wish to keep the geraniums and begonias follow the instructions on page 127.

123 A SUN LOVING BOX

This is simple to plant, easy to look after but it needs lots of sun to make it look so pretty.

Site
Window ledge; full sun.

Container
Large terracotta window box: 80cm (32″) long, 20cm (8″) wide, 17½cm (7″) deep.

Plant
End May to early June.

In flower
End June to September.

Ingredients
5   various coloured gazanias *Gazania* x *hybrida*.
1   strip of Livingstone daisies to edge the box *Mesembryanthemum criniflorum*.
25 litres John Innes No 2 soil.
Broken pieces of polystyrene as drainage material.

Method
1. Cover the base of the container with 2½cm (1″) drainage material and add enough soil to bring the level to within 2½cm (1″) of the rim of the box.
2. Plant the gazanias spaced out along the middle of the box.
3. Carefully separate the Livingstone daisies, and plant along the front of the box so that they will spread over the edge.
4. Make sure the container looks well balanced and that all the plants are firmly in place, filling any remaining gaps with soil.
5. Water well. Add more soil if necessary.

Aftercare
This is an easy, generally trouble free box. Water regularly, although the Livingstone daisies prefer to be on the dry side. The gazanias need only an occasional liquid feed (not before the Livingstone daisies are in flower). But what they both ask for is lots of sun!

At the end of the Summer discard the Livingstone daisies and the gazanias unless you wish to try to overwinter the latter at temperatures 5–7°C (45–50°F).

124 BRIGHT AND CHEERFUL

The combination of red, yellow and blue never fails to catch the eye. Here is a simple planting that is cheap, cheerful and easy to look after.

Site
A sunny window ledge.

Container
Medium wooden window box (with a plastic liner): 55cm (22″) long, 15cm (6″) wide, 12½cm (5″) deep.

Plant
Mid to end May.

In flower
June to September.

Ingredients
1 strip of lobelia *Lobelia erinus* 'Mrs Clibran'.
1 strip or 6 plants of dwarf single French marigold *Tagetes tenuifolia* 'Lemon Gem'.
1 strip or 6 plants of salvia *Salvia splendens* 'Blaze of Fire', height 30cm (12″).
9 litres John Innes No 2 soil or a peat-based compost.
Small pieces of polystyrene as drainage material.

Method
1. Cover the base of the container with 2½cm (1″) drainage material and add 7½cm (3″) soil.
2. Alternate the salvias and tagetes in two rows at the front and back of the box.
3. Divide the lobelia and plant along the front edge and sides of the box.
4. Make sure the container looks well balanced and that all the plants are firmly in place, filling any remaining gaps with soil.
5. Water well. Add more soil if necessary.

Aftercare
Water regularly, and feed occasionally. You should not be troubled by greenfly, etc but if they do appear then spray accordingly. At the end of the season discard all the plants.

125 SUMMER COLOUR IN A PREDOMINANTLY FOLIAGE BOX

Here is the summer version of Recipe 58. Space between the foliage plants is limited but with careful attention to food and water the result can be very satisfactory.

Site
Window ledge, sunny aspect.

Container
Medium terracotta window box: 45cm (18") long, 20cm (8") wide, 15cm (6") deep.

Plant
Mid to end May.

In flower
From time of planting until end September.

Ingredients
2 small pale pink ivy leaf geraniums *Pelargonium* 'Sugar Baby', chosen for its lime green foliage and small but profuse flowers.
3 pink trailing ivy leaved geraniums *Pelargonium* 'Miss Liver Bird'.
½ strip of upright pale blue lobelia *Lobelia erinus* 'Cambridge Blue'.
½ strip of white alyssum *Lobularia maritima* 'Little Dorrit'.
1 slow growing conifer; this is a dwarf Lawson cypress *Chamaecyparis lawsoniana* 'Ellwoodii'.
2 variegated shrubs *Euonymus japonicus* 'Aureo pictus'.
2 ivies *Hedera helix* 'Chicago'.
10 litres John Innes No 2 soil.
Small pieces of polystyrene as drainage material.

Method
1. Assuming that you are starting entirely from scratch, cover the base of the container with 2½cm (1") drainage material and add 5cm (2") soil. If you already have an established foliage window box remove all the plants, and follow the instructions as given, substituting your own foliage plants. Take this opportunity to change the soil now and trim the roots of the ivies.
2. Plant the conifer in the centre, and the euonymus at either end of the box. Don't be afraid to prune the euonymus or any other shrubs you might use in order to keep the box uniform and neat.
3. Trim the roots of the established ivies and plant on either side of the centre, trailing over the front of the box.
4. Plant the two 'Sugar Baby' geraniums, one on either side of the conifer behind each ivy.
5. Plant the two 'Miss Liver Bird' geraniums at each end of the box in front of the two euonymus.
6. Carefully divide the lobelia and plant in three groups along the front of the box, and put a group in each rear corner.
7. Tuck two plants of alyssum in the front of the box on either side of the centre lobelia.
8. Make sure the container looks well balanced and that all the plants are firmly in place, filling any remaining gaps with soil.
9. Water well. Add more soil if necessary.

Aftercare
Take great care to water daily as there are a lot of plants in a small space and they need a regular supply of moisture. Feed and spray for greenfly, etc once a week.

Deadhead flowers on the geraniums. In the Autumn, remove the Summer bedding. Discard the lobelia and the alyssum. If you wish, the geraniums may be over-wintered, see page 127.

126 SIMPLE BEGONIAS

Begonias are a good subject for a window box. What is more they will thrive even on a north facing window ledge.

Site
Window ledge with sun or shade.

Container
Medium window box (wooden with a plastic liner): 55cm (22″) long, 15cm (6″) wide, 12½cm (5″) deep.

Early preparation
If you want to use begonia tubers – they will work out cheaper and you will find a better choice of colour – purchase in February or March at the latest (see page 127).

Plant
End May.

In flower
Mid June until end September.

Ingredients
3 non stop pink begonias, *Begonia* x *tuberhybrida*.
4 coleus plants *Coleus blumei*.
1 strip of trailing lobelia *Lobelia erinus* 'Blue Cascade'.
9 litres soil; preferably a peat-based compost although John Innes No 2 could also be used.
Small pieces of polystyrene as drainage material.

Method
1. Cover the base of the container with 2½cm (1″) drainage material and add 5cm (2″) soil.
2. Space the three begonias along the length of the box, if one of them is bigger than the others save it for the centre.
3. Plant two coleus plants at the back of the box so that they can be seen from inside the house, and two at either end.
4. Carefully divide the lobelia and plant around the sides and front of the box.
5. Make sure the container looks well balanced and that all the plants are firmly in place, filling any remaining gaps with soil.
6. Water well. Add more soil if necessary.

Aftercare
The box should be watered regularly, as rain water will not penetrate the large flat begonia leaves which act rather like an umbrella. Use a long spouted watering can to get between the leaves. Once flowering has begun give the plants a fortnightly liquid feed.

Remove all fading begonia flowers. Nip out the flower spikes of the coleus, and also the leading shoots to keep the plant bushy. By late Autumn the begonia leaves will begin to turn yellow. Discard the lobelia and coleus. You may keep the begonias through the Winter (see page 127).

127 SOMETHING FOR SHADE

The fuchsias and busy lizzies create a pastel mound together and don't seem to mind their shady home one bit.

Site
A shady window ledge.

Container
Large window box: 85cm (34″) long, 20cm (8″) wide, 17½cm (7″) deep.

Plant
End May.

In flower
June to late September.

Ingredients
8 busy lizzies of mixed colours *Impatiens* F1 hybrids (3 purple, 3 pink, 2 white).
2 white fuchsias *Fuchsia* 'Igloo Maid'.
4 silver foliage plants *Senecio cineraria (Cineraria maritima)*.
25 litres John Innes No 2 soil.
Small pieces of polystyrene as drainage material.

Method
1. Cover the base of the container with 2½cm (1″) drainage material and add 5cm (2″) soil.
2. Plant the front of the box from left to right as follows; purple busy lizzie, fuchsia, pink busy lizzie, fuchsia, purple busy lizzie.
3. At the back of the box from left to right plant: pink, white, purple, white and then pink busy lizzie.
4. In the centre, space the four silver cinerarias.
5. Make sure that all the plants are firmly in place, filling any remaining gaps with soil.
6. Water well. Add more soil if necessary.

Aftercare
These plants are thirsty drinkers and need watering regularly. Feed once a week as soon as the fuchsias begin to flower.

Beware of greenfly, etc on the fuchsias and spray routinely once a week. Remove dead fuchsia flowers. At the end of the Summer discard the busy lizzies and cinerarias.

If you wish to keep the fuchsias, pot them up, bring them indoors and gradually reduce their water supply. Leave them in a frost free place until the Spring when they can begin growth again.

128 SMART AND SOPHISTICATED

This marbled box looks good with just a simple arrangement of red flowers. An easy theme but an effective one.

Site
A formal setting on a smart window sill. Sunny aspect preferred.

Container
Large window box (marble painting on wood): 97½cm (39″) long, 20cm (8″) deep, 20cm (8″) wide.

Plant
Mid to end May.

In flower
From time of planting until September.

Ingredients
3 upright variegated leaf geraniums *Pelargonium* 'Caroline Schmidt'.
4 strong upright red geraniums *Pelargonium* 'Brunswick Orange'.
5 *Begonia semperflorens* of which 2 white with green foliage and 3 red with purplish brown foliage.
36 litres John Innes No 2 soil.
Crocks or pieces of broken polystyrene as drainage material.

Method
1. Cover the base of the container with 2½cm (1″) drainage material and add 7½cm (3″) soil.
2. Plant the three 'Caroline Schmidt' geraniums along the front of the box, with the four 'Brunswick Orange' geraniums behind them, (so that they can be seen through the spaces).
3. Plant the two white begonia semperflorens at each end of the box, and plant the three reds besides the three 'Caroline Schmidts'.
4. Make sure the container looks well balanced and that all the plants are firmly in place, filling any remaining gaps with soil.
5. Water well. Add more soil if necessary.

Aftercare
Water regularly and apply a liquid feed at the beginning of July and August. Spray for greenfly, etc if necessary.

Deadhead the geraniums. In the Autumn, discard the begonias. Follow the instructions on page 127 if you wish to keep the geraniums.

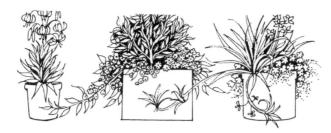

MISCELLANEOUS
POTS, TUBS AND BARRELS

129 SMALL LILY POT

These vibrant orange lilies combine well with the tall green flowered tobacco plants.

Site
Sunny.

Container
Terracotta pot; 45cm (18″) in diameter, 30cm (12″) deep.

Early preparation
The tobacco plant is easy to grow from seed. Buy seeds in early Spring and follow the instructions on the packet. (Mixed colours are easy to buy as plants in May – not so the green flowered ones.) Plant the lilies in 15cm (6″) pots of John Innes No 2 on purchase in January or February or buy them in growth in May.

Plant
Mid to end May.

In flower
It should begin to look good from July onwards.

Ingredients
  4 orange lilies *Lilium* 'Enchantment'.
  7 tobacco plants *Nicotiana alata* 'Lime Green'; 75cm (30″) high.
37 litres John Innes No 2 soil.
Pieces of polystyrene as drainage material.

Method
1. Cover the base of the pot with 5cm (2″) of drainage material.
2. Add soil until the level comes within 2½cm (1″) of the rim.
3. Plant six tobacco plants in a circle near the edge of the barrel, and plant one in the centre.

4. Make four holes for the lilies, so that they will form a circle slightly smaller than that of the tobacco plants. Empty them out of their pots and quickly transfer to their Summer home. Draw up the soil around each lily.
5. Make sure that the container looks well balanced and that all the plants are firmly in place.
6. Water well.

Aftercare
Water regularly and give an occasional liquid feed once flowering has become established.
  Spray for greenfly, etc as a matter of routine once a week. Transfer the lilies to the garden at the end of the Summer where they may continue dying back. Discard the tobacco plants.

130 A BARREL OF LILIES

This is a striking combination of yellows and blue which will continue to give weeks of pleasure even when the lily flowers are over.

Site
Sunny.

Container
Wooden half barrel or large pot: 60cm (24″) in diameter, 40cm (16″) deep.

Early preparation
Plant the lilies singly in 15cm (6″) pots immediately on purchase in January or February.

Plant
Mid to end May.

In flower
The yellow marguerites will flower throughout the Summer; the lilies will flower in July; and the morning glory will flower in July and August using the lilies as supports.

Ingredients
    4 lilies *Lilium* 'Citronella'; some of these will reach over 1 metre (3 feet) and will require staking.
    3 yellow daisy-like marguerites *Chrysanthemum frutescens* 'Jamaica Primrose'.
    3 morning glory *Ipomoea* 'Heavenly Blue'.
100 litres John Innes No 2 soil.
Pieces of polystyrene as drainage material.

Method
1. Cover the base of the container with 5cm (2″) drainage material and add 15cm (6″) soil.
2. Make a hole for each lily (so that they can be planted straight in) to form a wide circle, with one hole in the centre.
3. Carefully empty the lilies out of their pots and plant. Draw up the soil around each lily and then plant the marguerites in between the three outer lilies.
4. The soil level should now be within 5cm (2″) of the rim.

5. Water well and add more soil if necessary.
6. In late June, when the morning glory becomes available, plant three of them besides the three outer lilies so that they can use them as climbing frames.
7. Water immediately after planting.

Aftercare
Water generously. In hot weather you should be prepared to water daily.

Deadhead the marguerites and morning glory each day. Remove any unsightly faded lily flowers. Spray against greenfly, chrysanthemum eel worm miners, etc as necessary. Give a fortnightly liquid feed from mid-July.

At the end of the Summer you should discard the marguerites and morning glory. The lilies may be lifted and planted out in the garden. Alternatively you might leave them in the barrel, but be careful not to harm them when you replant for the Spring.

131 SUMMER PLANTING IN A CONIFER BARREL

This Summer planting scheme of white with hints of yellow provides a welcome lift to the dark tones of the conifer.

Site
Partial shade.

Container
Wooden half barrel: 60cm (24″) in diameter and 42½cm (17″) deep.

Plant
Mid to end May.

In flower
It should begin to look good from mid June onwards.

Ingredients
1 central slow-growing conifer *Chamaecyparis lawsoniana* 'Ellwoodii'; this has been in the barrel for 10 years.
3 creeping Jenny *Lysimachia nummularia;* these have also been established around the edge of the barrel for a few years.
5 tall, white, daisy-like marguerites *Chrysanthemum frutescens.*
5 small, white daisy-like marguerites such as *Chrysanthemum parthenium.*
1 strip of white lobelia, *Lobelia erinus* 'White Lady'.
A small amount of John Innes No 2 soil.

Method
As with the Winter example on page 79 I shall assume you already have a container with a large established conifer or small tree in the centre. As it would be impractical to replant the whole pot each season, you can just replant the outer edge. If the soil level has been allowed to fall, as so often is the case, use this opportunity to top up with new John Innes No. 2 soil, bringing the level to within 2½cm (1″) of the rim.
1. Make ten 7½cm (3″) deep holes for the marguerites around the conifer so that the tall ones can be planted at the back and the small ones can be put in between them at the front.
2. Carefully divide the strip of lobelia and plant around the edge of the barrel in between the creeping Jennies.
3. Make sure the plants are firmly in place. Water well and add more soil if necessary.

Aftercare
Water generously: in hot weather you must be prepared to do this daily. Give an occasional liquid feed from early July onwards.
Spray for chrysanthemum leaf miner, greenfly, etc as necessary. Deadhead all fading flowers. At the end of the Summer discard the marguerites and lobelia and then replant for the Winter.

132 SUMMER DELIGHT

This is simple to plant, and will delight all Summer long. The colours can be changed, of course, but the contrast of white and purple petunias is a good one, particularly when seen against the lime green helichrysum which by the end of the Summer will have made a lot of growth and will really show off the petunias well.

Site
Sunny.

Container
Medium sized pot: 35cm (14″) in diameter, 30cm (12″) deep.

Plant
Mid to end May.

In flower
May or June onwards.

Ingredients
4 *Petunia* x *hybrida*, of which 2 white and 2 purple.
1 *Helichrysum petiolatum* 'Limelight'.
25 litres John Innes No 2 soil.
Small pieces of polystyrene as drainage material.

Method
1. Cover the base of the pot with 5cm (2″) drainage material and add enough soil to bring the level to within 2½cm (1″) of the rim.
2. Plant the helichrysum in the middle.
3. Plant the four petunias (alternating white and purple) close to the edge so that they form an informal circle.
4. Firm down all the plants well into the soil.
5. Water well. Add more soil if necessary.

Aftercare
Water generously. In hot weather you must be prepared to do it daily, but it is best done either in the morning or late evening to avoid scorching the leaves. Use a long spouted watering can without a rose on the end so that you can get in between the foliage and avoid wetting, and so spoiling, the flowers.

Deadhead all fading flowers. Greenfly is a problem with petunias. Watch out for it and spray whenever necessary. At the end of the Summer you should discard the petunias and the helichrysum.

133 A POT FOR MID TO LATE SUMMER

You can choose a mixture of colours or just one. Either way this will be a bright display from late June onwards.

Site
Sunny.

Container
Almost any medium or large pot would be appropriate, this is a 'Florentine Square' pot: 30cm (12″) cubed.

Plant
Mid to end May.

In flower
It should begin to look good from early July onwards.

Ingredients
 4 dwarf bedding dahlias; any mixture of colours.
 4 coleus *Coleus blumei*; there are some beautiful different leaf markings to choose from.
25 litres John Innes No 2 soil.
Small pieces of polystyrene as drainage material.

Method
1. Cover the base of the container with 5cm (2″) drainage material and add enough soil to bring the level to within 7½cm (3″) of the rim.
2. Place one dahlia in each corner and a coleus in between.
3. Add soil around each plant, firm down, and fill any remaining gaps with soil to bring the level to within 2½cm (1″) of the rim.

Aftercare
Water generously. In hot weather you must be prepared to do it daily. Once flowering is well established the pot would benefit from an occasional liquid feed.

Spray for greenfly, blackfly, etc once a week or more often if necessary. Remove all spent dahlia flowers to prevent seedheads forming.

Nip out the flower spikes on the coleus plants so that they remain bushy. Wait until early frosts blacken the dahlias and then discard all the plants.

134 SUMMER GLORY

This is a traditional Summer planting with red geraniums, busy lizzie, lobelia and alyssum. The effect is very bright and cheerful.

Site
Sun or partial shade.

Container
Medium to large pot: 42½cm (17″) diameter and 42½cm (17″) deep.

Plant
Mid to end May.

In flower
End May onwards.

Ingredients
  4 upright red geraniums *Pelargonium* 'Cabaret'.
  1 variegated leaf geranium *Pelargonium* 'Caroline Schmidt'.
  4 salmon-pink busy lizzies *Impatiens* F1 hybrid.
  1 strip of white alyssum *Lobularia maritima* 'Little Dorrit'.
  1 strip of pale blue upright lobelia *Lobelia erinus* 'Cambridge Blue'.
  ½ strip of dark blue upright lobelia *Lobelia erinus* 'Crystal Palace'.
  60 litres John Innes No 2 soil.
  Crocks or small pieces of polystyrene as drainage material.

Method
1. Cover the base of the container with 5cm (2″) drainage material and add enough soil to bring level to within 7½cm (3″) of the rim.
2. Plant the variegated leaf geranium in the centre.
3. Plant the four red geraniums in a wide circle, alternating each with a busy lizzie.
4. Divide the alyssum and lobelia and plant alternatively around the edge of the container.
5. Make sure all the plants are firmly in place and that the display looks well balanced. Fill in any gaps with soil.
6. Water well and add more soil if necessary.

Aftercare
Water regularly, especially in hot weather when a daily check should be made. Apply a liquid feed once every two weeks from the end of June. Spray against greenfly, etc as necessary.

Deadhead the geraniums. Discard lobelia, alyssum, busy lizzies at the end of the flowering period. If you wish to over-winter the geraniums follow the instructions on page 127.

135 SUMMER PLANTING IN A VERSAILLES TUB

This is a simple Summer arrangement to take over from the Spring one we saw earlier. The busy lizzies are easy to look after and will go on flowering until October. At that stage they could be replaced by cyclamen and solanum.

Site
Any.

Container
Square Versailles tub: 37½cm (15″) cubed. Any medium to large barrel or pot would suit.

Plant
Late May or early June.

In flower
From time of planting until October.

Ingredients
  1 golden cupressus, *Cupressus macrocarpa* 'Gold-crest'; this is at least 42½cm (17″) tall which adds central height.
  2 variegated ivies *Hedera helix* 'Goldchild'.
  1 coleus *Coleus blumei*; choose one for its interesting leaf colour.
  3 red or pink variegated busy lizzies *Impatiens* 'New Guinea Hybrid'.
40 litres of John Innes No 2 soil or a peat-based compost.
Pieces of polystyrene as drainage material.
Plastic sheeting to line the tub.

Method
1. The bottom of a Versailles tub has moveable slats. Either use a rigid plastic liner or cut up some plastic sheeting to fit. Make sure it has at least six 2½cm (1″) slits to allow for drainage.
2. Cover the liner with 5cm (2″) drainage material, then top up with soil leaving about 10cm (4″) clear at the top.
3. Position the ivies in the front two corners of the tub with the cupressus at the centre back.
4. Plant the coleus in front of the cupressus.
5. Plant two busy lizzies behind each ivy, and one in the centre front.

6. Make sure the container is well balanced and that all the plants are firmly in place, filling any remaining gaps with soil.
7. Water well. Add more soil if necessary.

Aftercare
Water regularly throughout the Summer and in hot weather be prepared to do it daily. After the end of June, apply a liquid feed every two weeks.

Nip out the flowering tip of the coleus as soon as it appears in order to retain a bushy plant. There should be no need to spray against insects or to deadhead.

At the end of the flowering period retain the ivies and cupressus and replant with Autumn colour or Spring bulbs. Discard the busy lizzies.

136 UNIFORMITY

Strawberry pots are best planted with something small which is in scale. Here we have used a mixture of blue and white ageratum, and blue lobelia which has mounded together beautifully to give a uniform display.

Site
Sunny sheltered position.

Container
Terracotta strawberry pot: 27½cm (11″) in diameter, 42½cm (17″) deep.

Plant
Mid to end May.

In flower
June until September.

Ingredients
1 strip of blue and 1 strip of white ageratum *Ageratum houstonianum*.
½ strip of pale blue upright lobelia *Lobelia erinus* 'Cambridge Blue'.
20 litres John Innes No 2 soil.
Coarse grit or finely broken polystyrene as drainage material.

Method
1. Cover the base of the container with 5cm (2″) drainage material.
2. To help drainage further, take a long cardboard tube and place it on its end in the centre of the pot. Surround it with soil to make it free standing; later on it will be filled with gravel and removed.
3. Bring the soil level up to the lowest hole and firm it down well.
4. Carefully separate the strips of plants, then, planting from the outside in, pass the roots of one of the plants through the lowest hole so that they rest on top of the soil.
5. Cover with soil, firm down and gradually work your way round and up the pot until you reach the top.
6. Fill the tube with gravel or small stones, and then remove carefully leaving a column of drainage up the centre of the pot.

7. The soil level should be within 2½cm (1″) of the rim.
8. Plant four ageratums in the top, along with two pale blue lobelias to spread over the edge at either side.
9. Check that all the plants are firmly in place, and that the soil in each hole is compacted. Failure to do so will result in the soil being washed away as you water.
10. Water well from all angles, but do it carefully in order to retain the soil.

Aftercare
Watering will be your main consideration. Ageratums are thirsty plants and dry soil will reduce their performance considerably. So take care to water regularly and thoroughly.

As the plants mature their roots will bind the soil and there will be less chance of spillage. Then the problem becomes how to get the water in the pot. This is where the special drainage tube becomes so important. It allows water to reach the bottom of the pot easily and should ensure moist soil.

The plants should remain free from greenfly, etc. Feed occasionally with a liquid fertiliser from the end of June onwards. Deadhead as the flowers fade. At the end of September discard all the plants.

137 A SUN LOVING STRAWBERRY POT

These bright little flowers love the warm dry home provided by this small strawberry pot.

Site
Full sun.

Container
Terracotta strawberry pot: 22½cm (9″) in diameter, 35cm (14″) deep.

Plant
Mid to end May.

In flower
June to August.

Ingredients
2 strips of Livingstone daisies *Mesembryanthemum criniflorum*.
1 strip of blue lobelia *Lobelia erinus* 'Cambridge Blue'.
13 litres John Innes No 2 soil.
Coarse grit or fine stones as drainage material.

Method
1. Cover the base of the container with 5cm (2″) drainage material.
2. To help drainage further, take a long cardboard tube and place it on its end in the centre of the pot. Surround it with soil to make it free-standing. Later on it will be filled with gravel and removed.
3. Bring the soil level up to the lowest hole and firm it down well.
4. Carefully separate the strips of plants, then, planting from the outside in, pass the roots of one of the plants through the lowest hole.
5. Continue round and up the pot until you reach the top, mixing lobelia and Livingstone daisies all the way round, sometimes putting the two plants in the same hole.
6. Bring the soil level within 2½cm (1″) of the rim.
7. Fill the tube with gravel or small stones, and then remove it carefully, leaving a column of fine drainage material in the centre of the pot.

8. Plant the lobelia at the top along with the last of the Livingstone daisies.
9. Check that the plants are all firmly in place, and that the soil in each hole is compact. Failure to do so will result in the soil being washed away as you water.
10. Water well from all angles, but do it carefully and slowly in order to retain the soil.

Aftercare
As the plants mature, watering will be less of a headache because the roots will bind the soil together in the holes. However, until then you will have to water with care.

Livingstone daisies like hot dry conditions best so water less than with other pots, but do not neglect. The lobelia will still like a drink.

Deadhead the Livingstone daisies regularly. At the end of the Summer discard all the plants.

138 ELEGANCE WITH FLOWERS

This pot has an elegant shape and lends itself to this wonderful display of geraniums tumbling down over drifts of lobelia which is planted through holes lower down in the pot.

Site
Sun or partial shade, but the sunnier the better.

Container
Terracotta strawberry pot: 22½cm (9″) in diameter, 42½cm (17″) deep.

Plant
Mid to late May onwards.

In flower
From time of planting until the frosts.

Ingredients
3 ivy leaf geraniums *Pelargonium* 'King of the Balkans'.
½ strip of upright dark blue lobelia *Lobelia erinus* 'Crystal Palace'.
16 litres John Innes No 2 soil.
Plenty of sharp grit or small stones as drainage material.

Method
1. Cover the base of the container with 5cm (2″) drainage material.
2. To help drainage further take a long cardboard tube and place it on its end in the centre of the pot. Surround it with soil, carefully firming the soil down as you work your way up to the lowest hole in the side of the pot.
3. Carefully separate the strip of lobelia, and, planting from the outside in, pass the roots through the holes so that they are resting on soil.
4. Cover with soil, firm down gently and fill the pot with soil, bringing the level to within 10cm (4″) of the rim.
5. Fill the tube with grit or small stones and then carefully remove it leaving a column of drainage material in the centre of the pot.

6. Plant the three geraniums so that they are trailing over the sides of the pot.
7. Plant the remaining lobelias in the top of the pot between the geraniums.
8. Make sure the pot looks well balanced and that all the plants are firmly in place, filling any remaining gaps with soil.
9. Water well but carefully so as to cause minimum spillage.
10. Add more soil if necessary.

Aftercare
Water regularly but with great care until the roots of the lobelia bind the soil together in the holes. Feed every fortnight from the end of June.

Deadhead all faded flowers. At the end of the Summer, discard the lobelia. If you wish to keep the geraniums through the Winter follow the instructions on page 127.

139 CLAY BASKET ARRANGEMENT

This is a colourful planting using just one begonia and two busy lizzies.

Site
Sun or shade.

Container
Clay ornamental basket: 25cm (10″) in diameter, 20cm (8″) deep.

Plant
End May onwards (you could start the begonia into growth from a tuber in February – see page 127).

In flower
June onwards until the first frosts.

Ingredients
1 pale pink non-stop begonia, *Begonia* x *tuber-hybrida*.
2 busy lizzies; one pale pink, one dark pink *Impatiens* F1 hybrids.
6 litres of peat-based compost.
Horticultural grit or crocks as drainage material.

Method
1. Cover the base of the container with 2½cm (1″) of drainage material and add 10cm (4″) of the peat-based compost.
2. Plant the begonia towards the front of the pot with the busy lizzies tucked in on either side so that they will grow into both parts of the basket.
3. Add more soil to bring the level to within 2½cm (1″) of the rim.
4. Water well. Add more soil if necessary and then raise off the ground.

Aftercare
Water regularly using a long spouted watering can so that you reach in between the dense foliage of the begonia. Apply a liquid feed once a week from end June.

You should have little trouble with pests. Remove unsightly begonia flowers when they have faded. In the Autumn discard the busy lizzies. If you wish to keep the begonia tuber follow the instructions on page 127.

140 JUST A LITTLE POT

Here is an unusual idea for a very small pot where the combination of soft greys and pinks creates an unusual colour scheme.

Site
Sun or partial shade.

Container
Small pot: 25cm (10″) in diameter, 20cm (8″) deep.

Plant
End May.

In flower
June to September.

Ingredients
3 echeveria, with tight grey rosettes (often sold in late Spring as house plants) *Echeveria secunda*.
1 small begonia; look for a pale pink one with yellow centres to the flowers *Begonia semperflorens*.
1 *Sedum sieboldii* 'Mediovariegatum'; spread up to 37½cm (15″).
8 litres John Innes No 2 soil.
Grit or small pieces of polystyrene as drainage material.

Method
1. Cover the base of the pot with 2½cm (1″) drainage material and add 7½cm (3″) soil.
2. Plant the sedum at the front, with the three echeverias completing the outer circle.
3. Plant the begonia in the centre.
4. Fill in the gaps with soil, firm down the plants and water well.

Aftercare
Apart from regular but careful watering (so as to avoid unnecessary splashing on the echeverias) this little pot should make few other demands until the Autumn. At this time, the begonia should be discarded.

The sedum should survive outdoors otherwise you might like to pot it up and keep in a frost-free place. The echeverias should definitely come indoors if you wish to keep them for another season. Keep only barely moist in Winter.

141 RICH FOLIAGE FOR A WALLPOT

The bright green leaves of the tolmiea just seem to tumble out of the wallpot and provide a lovely contrast to the crimson geraniums.

Site
Sun or partial shade.

Container
Wallpot: 25cm (10″) long, 15cm (6″) wide, 20cm (8″) deep.

Plant
Mid to end May.

In flower
End May until September.

Ingredients
2 trailing ivy leaf geraniums *Pelargonium* 'Yale'.
1 crimson red upright geranium *Pelargonium* 'Cabaret'.
1 pig-a-back plant *Tolmiea menziesii*; little plantlets develop at the end of older leaves, hence its common name.

5 litres John Innes No 2 soil.
Small pieces of polystyrene as drainage material.

Method
1. Cover the base of the wallpot with 2½cm (1″) drainage material and add 5cm (2″) of soil.
2. Plant the two geraniums on either side of the pot.
3. Plant the tolmiea at the centre front and the upright geranium behind.
4. Make sure the container looks well balanced and that all the plants are firmly in place, filling any remaining gaps with soil.
5. Water well. Add more soil if necessary.

Aftercare
Water generously: in hot weather you must be prepared to do it daily. Give a liquid feed every two weeks from July onwards.

Spray for greenfly, etc as a matter of habit once a week. At the end of the Summer you should dismantle the wallpot.

You can overwinter the geraniums indoors (see page 127), but the tolmiea is hardy and so can be planted out in the garden.

142 SMALL BUT COLOURFUL

There is not much planting space in this wallpot but that need not stop us producing a small but colourful display.

Site
Sun or shade.

Container
A small terracotta wallpot: 30cm (12″) long, 10cm (4″) wide, 20cm (8″) deep.

Plant
Mid to end May.

In flower
It should begin to look good from mid June onwards.

Ingredients
2 red busy lizzies *Impatiens* F1 hybrids.
1 variegated ivy *Hedera helix* 'Goldchild'.
4 litres John Innes No 2 soil.
Horticultural grit or small pieces of polystyrene as drainage material.

Method
1. Cover the base of the wallpot with 2½cm (1″) drainage material and add 5cm (2″) soil.
2. Plant the ivy in the centre of the pot so that it trails over the front.
3. Plant the two busy lizzies at either end of the pot.
4. Fill in the gaps with soil; make sure the plants are firmly in place; water well and if necessary add more soil. But beware, don't bring the level too high or else it will spill over the top.

Aftercare
Water carefully: in hot weather you must be prepared to do it daily. You should give a liquid feed every week.

The busy lizzies should continue flowering well into September and even October. Then discard. The ivy can be used again for another display.

143 SPIDER PLANT WALLPOT

A simple but attractive idea for a wallpot.

Site
Sunny.

Container
Terracotta wallpot:
22½cm (9″) long,
17½cm (7″) wide,
17½cm (7″) deep.

Plant
Mid to end May.

In flower
From time of planting until end September or later.

Ingredients
1 spider plant *Chlorophytum comosum* 'Mandaianum'.
2 pink geraniums *Pelargonium* 'Cal'.
3 plants of white alyssum (less than ½ strip) *Lobularia maritima* 'Little Dorrit'.
6 litres of John Innes No 2 soil.
Small pieces of polystyrene as drainage material.

Method
1. Cover the base of the wallpot with 2½cm (1″) drainage material and add 5cm (2″) soil.
2. Plant the spider plant in the centre and the two pink geraniums on either side.
3. Plant the alyssum around the front and sides.
4. Make sure the plants are firmly in place and fill in the gaps with soil.
5. Water well. Add more soil if necessary.

Aftercare
Water carefully but regularly and in hot weather be prepared to do it daily as wallpots can dry out very quickly. Give a liquid feed once a fortnight from the middle of July.

Deadhead the geraniums, and spray against aphids if necessary.

As the Summer progresses the spider plant should send out little runners which will eventually trail. In the Autumn when you are dismantling the pot these can be detached, potted up and brought indoors with the parent plant for the Winter. If you wish to keep the geraniums follow the instructions on page 127.

URNS, PEDESTALS AND CHIMNEY POTS

144 FRAGRANT AND PRETTY

This verbena is a delightful shade of pink and makes a lovely subject for this unusual marble urn.

Site
Sun or partial shade, near enough for you to enjoy the delicious scent.

Container
This is a marble cast urn: 22½cm (9″) in diameter, with a planting depth of 22½cm (9″).

Plant
Mid to end May.

In flower
From time of planting until late Summer.

Ingredients
1 verbena *Verbena* x *hybrida* 'Sissinghurst'.
½ strip of pale blue lobelia *Lobelia erinus* 'Cambridge Blue'.
9 litres John Innes No 2 soil, although if you manage to find a well-established verbena then you will need much less.
Small pieces of polystyrene as drainage material.

Method
1. Cover the base of the urn with 2½cm (1″) drainage material and add enough soil so that when planted the verbena will sit just beneath the rim of the container.
2. Plant the verbena and bring up the soil level around the sides.
3. Separate the lobelia and tuck it in around the verbena. Firm down all the plants.
4. Water well.

Aftercare
Water with care so that the water soaks into the urn. In hot weather you should be prepared to water daily, either in the early morning or evening.

Deadhead to prolong the flowering period. Stake discreetly if necessary. Discard at the end of the Summer.

145 THE AGAVE URN

This is a beautiful urn which lends itself to the stately shape of the agave.

Site
Sunny.

Container
Cast iron urn: 40cm (16″) in diameter, 52½cm (21″) deep, although the planting depth is only 25cm (10″).

Plant
Early June.

In flower
The ageratum will flower from June to September, the agave is used here as a foliage plant. It only flowers after many years and then dies.

Ingredients
1 agave *Agave americana* 'Marginata' with its rosette of sword-like leaves each with a spiky tip.
4 mid-blue ageratum *Ageratum houstonianum.*
1 litre of John Innes No 2 soil. We are presuming, as in this case, that the agave itself has a well-established root system and therefore the pot will need very little extra soil.
Crocks or pieces of polystyrene as drainage material.
A piece of black plastic to use as a liner.

Method
1. Line the container with a piece of black plastic to protect it from contact with moisture from the soil. (This would be unnecessary with a modern terracotta or plastic urn.)
2. Put 2½cm (1″) drainage material at the base of the planting area and add 2½cm (1″) soil, depending on size of the agave root system.
3. Plant the agave so that the base of the plant is just below the rim of the container.
4. Plant the ageratum in between the leaves near the edge of the urn so that it will form a good frill.
5. Check that the agave is in the centre, and that all the plants are firmly in position.
6. Fill any gaps with soil, and water well.

Aftercare
The ageratum will soon tell you when it needs a drink, so water regularly.

Deadhead throughout the summer. You should not be troubled with aphids. In the Autumn repot the agave in John Innes No 2 soil and bring it indoors into a frost free environment. Keep it in a conservatory, or beneath the staging in a greenhouse, or treat it as a houseplant. Only beware, it has very sharp spines on the end of its leaves. Discard the ageratum.

146 A PEDESTAL OF SOFT PINKS

This is a dainty arrangement of soft pinks and greys.

Site
Sun or partial shade.

Container
Pedestal and Urn. Urn: 30cm (12″) in diameter, 22½cm (9″) deep. Pedestal: 42½cm (17″) high.

Plant
Mid to end May.

In flower
From time of planting until first frosts.

Ingredients
5 pink geraniums of which 2 *Pelargonium* 'Mme Crousse' (a lovely soft pink trailer); 2 *Pelargonium* 'Sweet Mimosa', soft pink, semi-prostrate with scented grey green leaves; 1 *Pelargonium* 'Party Dress', one of the pink Irenes.
2 purple and white trailing fuchsias *Fuchsia* 'Eva Borg'.
1 *Helichrysum* "microphyllum", used purely as a foliage plant.
1 *Senecio cineraria (Cineraria maritima)* with delicate silver leaves.
1 dark purple verbena *Verbena* x *hybrida*.
1 strip of pale blue lobelia *Lobelia erinus* 'Cambridge Blue'.
1 pot of white lobelia *Lobelia erinus* 'Snowball'.
9 litres John Innes No 2 soil.
Small pieces of polystyrene as drainage material.

Method
1. Cover the base of the container with 2½cm (1″) drainage material and add 5cm (2″) soil.
2. Plant the two 'Mme Crousse' at the front of the urn, with the white lobelia in the middle.
3. Plant 'Party Dress' at the centre back and then plant 'Sweet Mimosa' on either side.
4. Plant the helichrysum, the cineraria and the verbena in the centre.
5. Plant the two fuchsias on either side of 'Mme Crousse' and then divide the blue lobelia and plant around the sides.
6. Make sure the container looks well balanced and that all the plants are firmly in place, filling any remaining gaps with soil. Water well. Add more soil if necessary.

Aftercare
There are a lot of plants in a very small area so regular watering is essential. Feed once a week from the end of June.

Spray for greenfly, etc as necessary and deadhead all faded flowers.

At the end of September you should pot up the pelargoniums and fuchsias, and bring them indoors (see page 127). Discard the other plants.

147 REGAL PINKS IN A PEDESTAL

Regal pelargoniums make a magnificent display in this pedestal. They look particularly good against the vivid green background of the heather and spider plants.

Site
Sheltered site in sun or light shade.

Container
Terracotta pedestal and bowl: this one has a 52½cm (21″) high pedestal and a 52½cm (21″) diameter, 20cm (8″) deep bowl.

Plant
End May.

In flower
June onwards.

Ingredients
1 strip of trailing lobelia *Lobelia erinus* 'Blue Cascade'.
1 strip of white alyssum *Lobularia maritima* 'Little Dorrit'.
3 regal pelargoniums *Pelargonium* 'Georgia Peach'; there are many others to choose from.
3 spider plants *Chlorophytum comosum* 'Mandaianum'.
1 large upright heather *Erica arborea* 'Albert's Gold', with vivid green foliage.
2 variegated ivies *Hedera helix* 'Sagittifolia Variegata'.
30 litres of peat-based compost.
Small pieces of polystyrene as drainage material.

Method
1. Cover the base of the container with 2½cm (1″) drainage material and add 7½cm (3″) soil.
2. Plant the heather in the centre of the bowl with the three spider plants spaced around.
3. Plant the regal pelargoniums in between the spider plants.
4. Plant the two ivies at the rim of the bowl behind two of the regal pelargoniums.
5. Carefully divide the strips of alyssum and lobelia and alternate them around the edge of the bowl.
6. Add more soil so that the level comes within 2½cm (1″) of the rim. Firm down all the plants. Make sure the pedestal looks well balanced.
7. Water well. Add more soil if necessary to fill any gaps.

Aftercare
Water generously. The bowl is quite shallow for this quantity of plants and in hot weather you must be prepared to water it daily. Give a liquid feed once every two weeks.

Spray for greenfly, etc as often as necessary. At the end of the Summer you can bring the regal pelargoniums indoors (see page 127). Discard the lobelia and alyssum, but replant the heather and ivies for the next seasonal display (see the example in Recipe 53).

148 BRIMMING OVER

Unlike the previous pedestal where individual plants were still clearly visible, this display has so developed that the flowers all mingle together.

Site
Sun or partial shade.

Container
Terracotta pedestal and bowl: 52½cm (21″) high pedestal with 52½cm (21″) diameter, 20cm (8″) deep bowl.

Plant
Mid to end May.

In flower
June till September.

Ingredients
1 strip of trailing lobelia *Lobelia erinus* 'Blue Cascade'.
½ strip of white alyssum *Lobularia maritima* 'Little Dorrit'.
4 ivy leaf geraniums *Pelargonium* 'Achievement'.
1 variegated scented leaf geranium *Pelargonium* 'Lady Plymouth'.
2 deep purple verbena *Verbena* x *hybrida*.
4 pink busy lizzies *Impatiens* F1 hybrids.
3 trailing fuchsias *Fuchsia* 'Magic Flute'; an elegant single flower with coral rose corolla and crisp white sepals.
30 litres John Innes No 2 soil.
Small pieces of polystyrene as drainage material.

Method
1. Cover the base of the bowl with 2½cm (1″) drainage material and add 7½cm (3″) of soil.
2. Plant the 'Lady Plymouth' geranium towards the centre back of the bowl with two 'Achievements' on either side near the rim, and the other two either side of the centre front, again near the rim.
3. Plant the fuchsias around the edge so that they will cascade in between the 'Achievements'.
4. Plant the busy lizzies in the central area of the bowl, along with the two verbenas.
5. Carefully divide the strips of lobelia and alyssum. Tuck the lobelia all the way around the edge of

the bowl, leaving just enough space for the alyssum to go on either side of the central fuchsia.
6. Fill in the gaps with soil, bringing the level to within 2½cm (1″) of the rim. Firm down all the plants. Check that the fuchsias and geraniums look well balanced.
7. Water well. Add more soil if necessary.

Aftercare
Water generously as this container is closely planted: in hot weather be prepared to do it daily. Apply a liquid feed in early July and August.

Spray for greenfly, etc as and when necessary. Deadhead all fading flowers.

At the end of the Summer discard the verbena, lobelia, busy lizzies and alyssum. You may bring the geraniums and fuchsias indoors (see page 127).

149 CHIMNEY POT MAGIC

It's hard to believe that this magnificent display is growing out of a small container wedged into the top of the chimney pot. Daily watering and regular feeding can produce amazing results.

Site
It must be able to enjoy the morning sun, as morning glory flowers open in the morning and close up in the evening, each one lasting only a day. It needs a warm sheltered position.

Container
A tall chimney pot with a small plastic or terracotta container which will sit snugly inside. Here we have used a pot 25cm (10″) in diameter, 22½cm (9″) deep.

Plant
Mid to end May, and add the morning glory from mid to end June.

In flower
May to September, although the morning glory will only flower from July.

Ingredients
4 trailing ivy leaved geraniums *Pelargonium* 'Yale'; there are many others to choose from. The important point to remember is to buy large plants so that they will be in proportion to the general scale of the display.
1 upright variegated leaf geranium *Pelargonium* 'Caroline Schmidt'.
1 strip of trailing lobelia *Lobelia erinus* 'Mixed' but any trailing lobelia would do.
1 large established variegated ivy *Hedera helix* 'Adam'. The longer the trails the better as in the early stages they are wound around the framework above the chimney pot.
2 petunias *Petunia* x *hybrida*, Grandiflora type.
2 morning glory *Ipomoea* 'Heavenly Blue'.
7 litres of John Innes No 2 soil.
Small pieces of polystyrene as drainage material.
A tall wire A-shaped frame to support the ivy and morning glory.

Method
1. Cover the base of the container with 2½cm (1″) drainage material and add 10cm (4″) of soil.
2. Fix the wire frame in position at the back of the pot.
3. Plant the ivy at the front of the pot and allow part of it to trail downwards and part to wind around the wire frame.
4. Plant the two trailing geraniums on each side of the ivy.
5. Plant the upright geranium 'Caroline Schmidt' in the centre of the container in front of the wire frame.
6. Plant the petunias either side of 'Caroline Schmidt', also in front of the wire frame.
7. Plant two empty flower pots behind the frame to take the morning glory.
8. Fill in the gaps with soil.
9. Carefully separate the strip of lobelia and plant it around the edge of the pot.
10. Water well. Add more soil if necessary.
11. Remove the empty pots towards the end of June and plant the morning glory, winding the long trails up both sides of the framework.

Aftercare
Water daily and give a weekly liquid feed. Spray against greenfly and other pests once a week as well. Deadhead all flowers as they fade. Continue to train the morning glory around the frame along with the ivy.

Before the first frosts, remove the geraniums and overwinter indoors (see page 127). Discard all the other plants except the ivy which may either be planted out in the garden or replanted for an Autumn display.

150 FUCHSIAS IN A CHIMNEY POT

These fuchsias look very graceful tumbling out of their chimney pot home. This is easy to plant and simple to look after.

Site
In sun or partial shade.

Container
A tall chimney pot with a small plastic or terracotta container which will fit snugly inside. This one is 25cm (10") in diameter, 22½cm (9") deep.

Plant
Mid May to June.

In Flower
From time of planting to end September.

Ingredients
2 large double red and white fuchsias *Fuchsia* 'Swingtime'.
2 white daisy-like marguerites *Chrysanthemum frutescens*.
10 litres John Innes No 2 soil.
Small pieces of polystyrene as drainage material.

Method
1. Cover the base of the container with 2½cm (1") drainage material and add 10cm (4") soil.
2. Plant the fuchsias opposite each other, either side of the pot so that the base of the plants are sitting just below the rim of the pot.
3. Plant the two marguerites in the gaps in between the fuchsias.
4. Make sure the container looks well balanced and that all the plants are firmly in place, filling any remaining gaps with soil.
5. Water well. Add more soil if necessary to bring the level to within 2½cm (1") of the rim.

Aftercare
Fuchsias are thirsty drinkers and need to be watered frequently. Give the pot a liquid feed once a week and at the same time spray against greenfly, etc. The marguerites could suffer from chrysanthemum leaf miner maggots and should be sprayed accordingly.

Deadhead all faded flowers so that the flowering period is lengthened. At the end of September remove the fuchsias from the container and pot into 15cm (6") pots. If you wish you can overwinter the fuschias indoors, see page 127. Discard the marguerites.

MAIL ORDER SPECIALISTS

This list is by no means exhaustive. For further names and addresses, look among the adverts in the garden magazines and in the Sunday newspapers.

Begonias, Geraniums, Ivies: Fibrex Nurseries Ltd, Honeybourne Road, Pebworth, Nr Stratford-on-Avon, CV37 8XT. Telephone: 0789 720788

Bulbs: Walter Blom and Son Ltd, Coombelands Nurseries, Leavesden, Watford, Hertfordshire WD2 7BH. Telephone: 09273 72071

Van Tubergen PO Box 74, Hull, HU9 1PQ. Telephone: 01031 2521 19030

Broadleigh Gardens, Bishops Hull, Taunton, Somerset TA4 1AE. Telephone: 0823 86231

Fuchsias: Jackson's Nurseries, Clifton Campville, Nr Tamworth, Staffordshire, B79 0AP. Telephone: 082786 307

Hardy Plants and Shrubs: David Austin, Bowling Green Lane, Albrighton, Wolverhampton, WV7 3HB. Telephone: 090722 2142

Herbaceous and Conifers: Bressingham Gardens, Diss, Norfolk, IP22 2AB. Telephone: 037988 464

Roses: R. Harkness and Co Ltd, The Rose Gardens, Hitchin, Herts. SG4 0JT. Telephone: 0462 34027

John Mattock, Nuneham Courtney, Oxford, OX9 9PY. Telephone: 086738 265

Seeds: Thompson and Morgan, London Road, Ipswich, Suffolk IP2 0BA. Telephone: 0473 688588

Shrubs: Notcutts, Woodbridge, Suffolk, IP12 4AF. Telephone: 03943 3344

Hillier Nurseries, Winchester, Hants, SO5 19PA. Telephone: 0794 68733

Marbled Window Boxes: Rosalind Lewis-Williams, 78 Cromwell Avenue, Highgate, London N6 5HQ. Telephone: 01-348 5662

182

INDEX TO INTRODUCTIONS

folios refer to *page* numbers

folios refer to *recipe* numbers